The Object of Reverie

The Object of Reverie: Appearance of the Uncreated Light

Within the ethereal abyss of dream and reason,
Light and Flame in time of shadow

ROBERT F. THOMPSON

Cover images:

"The Crystal Ball" (1902) by John William Waterhouse
Photo in the public domain

Salvatore Mundi (c. 1500) by Leonardo da Vinci
Photo in the public domain

Art Deco object from a
Greenwich Village antiques shop,
New York City.
Photo by the author.

Cover design by the author

Clip art from
Florida Center for Instructional Technology (FCIT)
http://fcit.usf.edu/

On the page of dedication,
the source of the lines from Robert Lax
is his poem, *A Song for Our Lady*.

Other titles by Robert F. Thompson:

Life-Giving Spring: The Eternal Fountain (2020)
Taliesin's Harp: A Poetics of the Divine-Humanity (2019)
The Anthropocosmic Vision: For a New Dialogic Civilization (2017)
From Glory to Glory: The Sophianic Vision of Fr. Sergius Bulgakov (2016)

A Perennials Study Group publication
Memphis, Tennessee

Printed by Kindle Direct Publishing
https://kdp.amazon.com

Veriditas

For
Juan J. Fuentes

And to the memory of three
wisdom teachers now on the other side:

Robert Lax (1915-2000)
"Everything that exists can turn to prayer;
even the water, even the air."

Murat Yagan (1915-2013)
teacher of "the art of living as a human"

John Moriarty (1938-2007)
in whom is Ireland

With thanks to
El Niño de Atocha
who turns suffering into joy

"There is only one way of truth,
but in it the streams flow together from different sides
as though into an eternal river."
— Clement of Alexandria (*Stromata*, Book I, Chapter 5)

Table of Contents

<h1 style="text-align:center"><u>Preface</u></h1>

A person picking up this book for the first time might wonder, "What kind of book is this?" It can perhaps be described as a text of "vernacular" *sapiential* (wisdom) literature arising out of an understanding of the Christian faith as melody, as fragrance, as pure poetry. The term *vernacular*, as used in academic circles, implies some type of cultural translation—where concepts are presented or rendered in contexts where they are not normally encountered.[1] This book can also be understood as performing a kind of cultural therapy. Readers of my previous books will be aware of the extent to which I have drawn on Russian or, more broadly, Central and East European Christian spiritual experience and tradition. This present book does so as well, although with a difference. This difference lies in authorial intent with regard to style. Unlike my previous books, I have hoped to write more of this book in the "first person." I have also hoped to explore the notion of reverie as manifested in writing. Most commonly, reverie appears in the English language as a noun. Reverie as we experience it, however, is dynamic—in motion, flow.[2] This flowingness characteristic of reverie connects with a long tradition in the West from the over-flowingness of the One in Plotinus, a tradition reflected much later in the fontality of Franciscan theology.

It is this dynamism of reverie that is intended when we coin an adverbial form of the word, *reveriesial*, which may not appear in any dictionary. What is *reveriesial* writing like? It is like drawing near to a fire. As fire is insubstantial yet sometimes seems to have a shape, it is

---

[1] "Vernacular theology" was a term coined by Ian Doyle in the 1950s and brought to prominence especially by Nicholas Watson and Bernard McGinn in the mid-1990s. A restricted usage of the term denoted medieval texts of Christian spiritual literature in the West that were neither Scholastic nor monastic. My use of "vernacular" is an expanded adaptation of the concept for contemporary expressions of Christian wisdom.

[2] Flow has been characterized as optimal experience, spontaneous thought, including dynamic cascade of insight, coupled with enhanced implicit learning. From John Vervaeke, Leo Ferraro, and Arianne Herrera-Bennett, "Flow as Spontaneous Thought: Insight and Implicit Learning," in Kalina Christoff and Kieran C. R. Fox, editors, *The Oxford Handbook of Spontaneous Thought: Mind-Wandering, Creativity, and Dreaming*, May 2018. Abstract on-line at: <https://www.oxfordhandbooks.com/view/10.1093/oxfordhb/9780190464745.001.0001/oxfordhb-9780190464745-e-8> (Accessed 9/12/2020)

not clear that reverie always has a discernable "object"—or at least not an empirical object.[3] The writing this present book is also intended to reflect a kind of "reasoning" in a space of freedom. The writing in this book is intended to explore how we deliberate—if not in adversarial mode, then … how? As reverie itself is experienced by us, the writing here may manifest in fragments or in a fragmentary way. These fragments may, like ephemeral flames of fire, remind readers of something they need to remember, if the Spirit wills it so.[4] Reverie, as understood in this book, is the name for all phenomenality whatsoever. As phenomenality as such, reverie is also the prism of the divine Light—the "uncreated light" in Orthodox Christian terminology. The writings of, for example, Jacob Boehme, in their symbolics, are emblematic of what I call reveriesial writing in this present text.

This book is also about "Babylon" and what it is like to be "leaving Babylon." This is a book about where we live now, including the regularity of "tending the roots" (as, perhaps, a kind of "Roots Christianity"). This book is also concerned with possible meanings of the words "prophet" and "prophetic" and other variants or synonyms. Fundamentally, this book is about divine illumination. The narrative of this book, in its unfolding, considers at some length the late Medieval Byzantine saint, Symeon the New Theologian, who has been referred to by Fr. John McGuckin as "prophet of the presence of God."[5]

---

[3] Reveriesial writing is not always "about" something, although it may be. Jesus said: "Truly I tell you, unless you change and become like children, you will never enter the kingdom of heaven." (Matthew 18:3, NRSV) Newborn children come into the world in states of reverie without objects (in the sense of foregrounds clearly distinguished from backgrounds). They are still in states of wonder—closer to the Kingdom. See, for example, Victoria Wisdom, "Reverie: A Portal to the Numinous—An Exploration into Early Childhood Psychospiritual Awareness," Ph.D. dissertation, 2014, Pacifica Graduate Institute. On-line at: <https://search.proquest.com/openview/ c681be30db0a8f583fac2685cd354796/> (Accessed 10/28/2020)

[4] Ancient rabbis spoke of the Torah given to Moses as written "in black fire on white fire."

[5] John McGuckin, "Symeon the New Theologian's *Hymns of Divine Eros*: A Neglected Masterpiece of the Christian Mystical Tradition," *Spiritus*, 5 (2005): 182–202, p. 182. On-line at: <https://academiccommons.columbia.edu/ download/fedora_content/download/ac:146165/content/5.2mcguckin.pdf> (Accessed 6/4/2020)

The glass sphere on the coffee table evokes within us an *"imagina-rium"* within which the fundamental realities manifest themselves. These realities include the cosmic Tree and the cosmic Fountain. The fountain was a key image in my book on the Blessed Virgin Mary. In this present book, the image that predominates in our *imaginarium* is the transfiguration of the fountain into flame of fire. In reflecting on this image we have further occasion to call our readers' attention to the life and work of Saint Symeon the New Theologian, for whom key spiritual concerns included—in addition to the divine light—the cosmic and interior fire, the situation of repentance (and associated tears) within the overall schema of Christian spiritual formation, and relation with one's elder or spiritual guide. This present book is not of the genre, *kephalia*, but can be understood as drinking from the same stream. I have always tried to direct my readers further "upstream" to sources from which I myself have learned something.

A classic text on the subject of reverie is, of course, Gaston Bachelard's *The Poetics of Reverie: Childhood, Language, and the Cosmos* that is a phenomenology of images, both in their making and in our witnessing of them. Mention can also be made of Ramon del Valle-Inclan's *The Lamp of Marvels: Aesthetic Meditations.* For background of all I am attempting in this present book, consult is the substantive work of Tom Cheetham, scholar of the creative imagination. I particularly commend his *Imaginal Love: The Meanings of Imagination in Henry Corbin and James Hillman* (Thompson, Connecticut: Spring Publications, 2015) as having particular relevance to the topic of reverie as it relates to the imaginal, more broadly. Reverie is about the deployment of images in relation to other images in ways that reveal something at risk of being forgotten. This is also an older way of doing philosophy—older than philosophy done by means of the deployment of concepts. The general topic of this present book on reverie has been of active interest for me at least since the mid-1970's at Yale Divinity School when I had conversations on the topic with Steve Osterman (d. 1986) who helped clarify the notion of reveriesial writing. With this book I offer him belated thanks.

Robert F. Thompson
March 21, 2021
Feast of the Transitus of St. Benedict

The Object of Reverie:
Appearance of the Uncreated Light

There the angel of the Lord appeared to him in a flame of fire out of a bush; he looked, and the bush was blazing, yet it was not consumed. Then Moses said, "I must turn aside and look at this great sight, and see why the bush is not burned up." When the Lord saw that he had turned aside to see, God called to him out of the bush, "Moses, Moses!" And he said, "Here I am." Then he said, "Come no closer! Remove the sandals from your feet, for the place on which you are standing is holy ground."
— Exodus 3:2-5 NRSV

Great are the accomplishments of faith, for the Three Holy Youths rejoiced in the fountain of flames as though in the waters of rest; and the prophet Daniel appeared, a shepherd to the lions as though they were sheep. So by their prayers, O Christ God, save our souls!
— Troparion (Tone 2)

When your pure heart was purged by the Spirit you became a vessel of clear prophecy; you saw things far away as though they were near at hand. When cast into their den you tamed the lions. Therefore, we honor you, blessed prophet, glorious Daniel.
— Kontakion (Tone 3)

What does the prophetic have to do with reverie? When the philosopher, theologian, and Iranologist, Henry Corbin (d. 1978), suggested that alchemy is the sister of prophecy (quoting the first imam of the Shi'ites),[6] I believe he was alluding to something about the nature of memory and of language. In this present book we will explore reverie as a function of memory and of language. Reverie, properly so-called, is the alchemical operation of transmuting idols into icons. Idols do not speak whereas icons reveal, to the attentive and attuned, a measure of the divine light that is within them and that is, in fact, within all beings. For Corbin, all the world is one vast iconostasis and all the

---

[6] Cheetham, *Imaginal Love*, p. 84.

world is an icon.[7] Reverie also serves the central task of our time, which is service as *midwife* to the birthing of a new culture that is planetary in its scope of vision—a culture that values our inherent rootedness both in heaven and in earth.

1.   The Seahorse

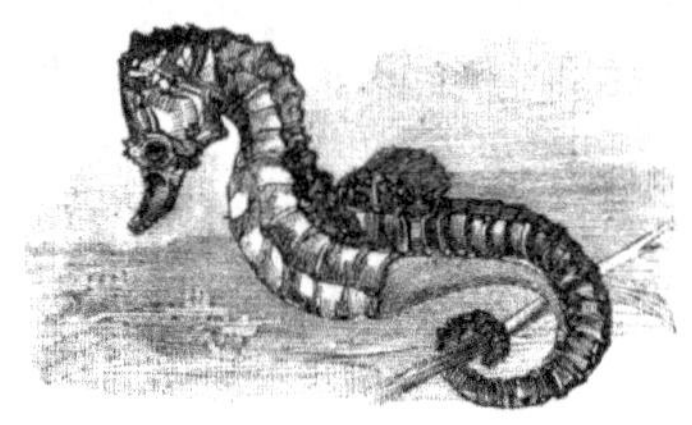

Souls know how to swim in Divine Light.
— Shaykh Nur al-Jerrahi

People used to, in some circles, talk about having a totem or "power animal"—an animal that held special affective significance for that person. For me, the little seahorse has always been especially appealing in that sense. The seahorse is a tiny creature, that doesn't call attention to itself. It lives in relatively shallow—but warm and sunny—waters near the shore. The poet, Robert Lax (d. 2000), wrote:

> The undersea vision, even at shallow depths, is
> almost narcotic, whatever is seen is seen with
> such peace, such composure. To look thus wide-
> eyed at all phenomena would surely be a kind of
> joy, a kind of psychic nourishment.[8]

---

[7] Cheetham, *Imaginal Love*, p. 129.

[8] Robert Lax, August 21, 1969, in "A Greek Journal," published in the book, *Love had a Compass*, edited by James J. Uebbing (New York: Grove Press, 1996), pp. 215-216. As quoted in a blog entry by Beth Cioffoletti at: <http://fatherlouie.blogspot.com/2007/03/lax-on-wisdom-part-two-under-water.html> (Accessed 1/14/2021). Also quoted in a book review by Lynn Jolly at: <http://www.thomasmertonsociety.org/Journal/23/23-1JollyRevGeorgiou.pdf> (Accessed 1/14/2021)

This is a manifestation of time in eternity and eternity in time—*sub specie aeternitatis*. The seahorse's tiny mouth resembles the tiny mouths typical of saints in Eastern Christian iconography.[9] In such icons "…there are no open mouths, no expression, and no actions. The mouth is small, meaning that the individual obeys the sacred commandments of God rather than speaking. The large forehead symbolizes teaching and knowledge. The large eyes are for seeing the uncreated light of God."[10] To inhabit this mode of life is to realize oneself as nobody—to gently lay down all of one's identities, save one.

The tiny seahorse manifests in its qualities what it is like to be attentively in the presence of the reveriesial object. By a process of free association from images of the seahorse, we might also be led to imagine the qualities of (other) horses. What are these qualities? From the time of childhood, we might have encountered "horses" at the carnival in the forms of a Merry-go-Round. In this form we encounter the horse that is not a horse that is the horse. Reverie is a type of improvisation.[11] The seahorse and, for example, the unicorn are each objects of reverie. The question of whether or not they "exist" in the physical/empirical realm is immaterial. Reverie has *imaginal* objects, some of which are also (like the seahorse) empirically embodied. We also find that reverie often begins in myth and typically returns to, or leads to, myth. Myth leads to reverie. If it is also the case that myth and reverie lead to metaphysics, the spiritual cosmology/metaphysics of G. I. Gurdjieff (d. 1949), has much to commend it. While this present book is not "about" Gurdjieff, one of the important wisdom teachers in the 20th century, some reference to his work will be made at various places in this book where it seems relevant.

---

[9] An icon is neither a representation nor an illustration. It is an evocation of the presence of a spiritual world. As an art form, it is both concrete and abstract.

[10] Iconographer, Randa Al Khoury Azar, as reported in a blog entry, "Khourieh Randa decodes the language of icons," by Karen Sullivan Sibert at her website, *aPennedPoint*, November 5, 2019. On-line at: <https:// apennedpoint.com/khourieh-randa-decodes-the-language-of-icons/> (Accessed 5/31/2020)

[11] Amanda Ravetz, "Sipping Water: Reverie and Improvisation," *Critical Studies in Improvisation / Études critiques en improvisation*, 2012, Volume 8, Number 2. On-line at: <https://www.criticalimprov.com/index.php/csieci/article/view/ 2139/2924> (Accessed 9/15/2020)

Besides the appearance of reverie in some literary productions, reverie has also been given a technical meaning in contemporary psychoanalysis. Psychoanalyst and writer, Thomas Ogden (Psycho-analytic Institute of Northern California), for example, seems to understand reverie as "a type of umbrella concept, which includes: somatic states; memories; associations; and counter-transference reactions."[12] Reverie is, for Ogden, the interplay of subjectivity and inter-subjectivity. For the British psychoanalyst, Wilfred Bion (d. 1979), reverie is compared to maternal attention to an infant—attention that both senses and anticipates the inner/outer movements of the child in a dreamlike state.[13] Within psychoanalysis, when both the analyst and the analysand allow themselves to enter into reverie there is movement not only into independent subjective states, but also into a shared inter-subjectivity. Another way of describing this "flow" state is by means of the term "transjectivity" (or "trans-subjectivity"). The psychologist, John Vervaeke (University of Toronto), has used this term as pointing to a conceptual shift beyond the subjective/objective binary.[14] From this perspective, we may come to understand *kenosis*, *theoria*, *theosis*, and *theurgy* as deeply interrelated.

For our purposes, however, reverie is simply the natural, contemplative, state of awareness that occurs when we allow ourselves to become silent and still. It is an attentiveness that is not purposeful. Anything whatsoever can become an object of reverie. Reverie is dynamic in the sense that attention to any object has the effect, in a state of reverie, of progressively expanding the context in which the object is appreciated. In other words, the *telos* or destination of reverie is apprehension of the object in its most comprehensive context possible—its apprehension *sub specie aeternitatis*, as it subsists in eternity,

---

[12] Fred Busch, "Searching for the analyst's reveries," *The International Journal of Psychoanalysis*, Volume 99, Number 3, 2018, pp. 569–589, pp. 573-574. On-line at: <https://sps.wildapricot.org/resources/Documents/Busch,%20 Searching%20for%20the%20analyst's%20reveries.pdf> (Accessed 6/22/2020)

[13] Ibid. This article by Fred Busch (Boston Psychoanalytic Society) is also a good introduction to the contributions of Wilfred Bion to the psychoanalytic uses of reverie.

[14] John Vervaeke in video conversation with Iain McGilchrist, facilitated and recorded by *Rebel Wisdom*, uploaded March 26, 2020. On-line at: <https:// youtu.be/JdB-BMdgFbk> (Accessed 9/11/2020). Vervaeke has also used this term in video conversation with Mark Vernon.

in God.[15] Any writing that has the effect of this same movement is what is meant, in this present text, by the term *reveresial writing.* It is often the case that the larger or more comprehensive context takes the form of story or myth.[16] Reverie expresses itself in myth. Reverie, in a profound sense, is our acceptance of, and entry into, death. The reveriesial process does not end there. It is also, as a psycho-spiritual process, the gateway into life. If reverie expresses itself in myth it is because the vertigo-producing (sleep or stupor-inducing) binary oppositions that we encounter in life threaten to overwhelm us. These manifestations cry out for harmonization. This is done through myth, which is a kind of reverie. In discussing the visionary work of the Russian writer, poet, and Christian mystic, Daniil Andreev (d. 1959), Larissa Koroleva writes:

> The whole universe of Daniil Andreev who interprets the natural and supernatural worlds, is built on pairs of antinomies such as good/bad, dark/light, divine/mundane. Such pairs that Claude Levi-Strauss called "binary oppositions" are essential for myth and, in his opinion, are a structural basis of myth. Clyde Kluckhohn, discussing some constant tendencies in myth-making, mentioned as "unarguable" "[d]uplication, triplication, and quadruplication of elements. (Levi-Strauss, 1955, suggests that the function of this repetition is to make the structure of the myth apparent.)" Not only the myth reveals the oppositions but also works towards resolving them by means of progresssive mediation. "[T]he purpose of myth is to provide a

---

[15] This is why reverie ultimately leads to sleep—falling asleep at the "feet" of the object of reverie. The impression of the "object" of reverie—seen in its reality, "in eternity"—is, in its power, overwhelming to the conscious mind, which "naturally" falls into sleep. This is what is so special about, for example, being somewhere outdoors far away from urban lights on a clear night and falling asleep while lying on one's back gazing up at the stars. On such special and rare occasions, from within this orb of Earth, one might even discern (or imagine that one discerns), in certain regions of the night sky, angelic intelligences in motion.

[16] See the understanding of myth in Norvene Vest, *Re-visioning Theology: A Mythic Approach to Religion* (Mahwah, New Jersey: Paulist Press, 2011).

logical model capable of overcoming a contradiction," states Levi-Strauss.[17]

From this perspective, the Holy Sophia or Holy Wisdom of some (Christian) sophiologies can also be understood as myth that mediates. In this case, Sophia mediates difference without opposition between the created and the uncreated worlds. The personalizing Holy Sophia is the "place" where the maximum exchange of energies between the heavenly realm and the earthly realm occurs. This place of the dynamic exchange of energies is also called *the imaginal.* The following poem by the Russian writer, poet and painter, Mikhail Lermontov (d. 1841), is a beautiful word-picture of this place where there is no opposition between the worlds—where there is unrestricted flow of energies between the worlds:

An angel flew through the midnight sky,
softly singing.
Moon, stars, clouds in a throng
listened to his holy song.

He sang of bliss of innocent spirits
sinless in paradise.
He sang of the great God,
his praise was unfeigned.

---

[17] Larissa Koroleva, "Daniil Andreev: The Mythology of *The Rose of the World,* 2002, Ph.D. dissertation, University of New South Wales (Australia), pp. 87-88. On-line at: <https://www.unsworks.unsw.edu.au/primo-explore/ fulldisplay/unsworks_64362/UNSWORKS> (Accessed 10/29/2020). The above excerpt from Koroleva's dissertation appears at the beginning of her section on "The Dichotomy of the Two Wills" where she discusses the centrality of polarities in Andreev's work. According to Koroleva, it is one of the tasks of *The Rose of the World* "to mediate the opposition between the ideal and the present state of the world." See the comments elsewhere in this present text regarding Karlfried Graf Durckheim's view of humankind as having dual origins.

In his arms he bore a young soul,
destined for the world of sorrow and tears.
And the sound of his song stayed forever
wordless and alive in that young soul.

Long that soul languished in the world
filled with a wonderful longing.
The earth's dull songs could not replace
the sounds of heaven for it.[18]

Reverie as understood in this present text seems to be a flow that may or may not have a particular focus. More importantly, reverie seems more likely to have both an occasion and a place where it occurs—a place conducive to the flow of insight, which may or may not be "inner visual" but may also be "inner auditory" or simply the fragments of reasonings that seem to have particular and especial interest.[19] Reveriesial writing, as the Lermontov poem illustrates, is not *about* the reverie but it is a "clear seeing" of reality beyond objectification that may issue from it. This clear seeing includes the discernment of the possibilities that attune with the divine melody in any given situation. Discernment of possibility as well as actuality enables creativity. The presence of venues of creativity is the criterion of human freedom.

Reverie is a mode of the flowingness of both light and life. In the following section we reflect on our experience of the world and the things and people in it as embodiments of light. Further in this present text we look to the roots of the ancient tradition of illuminism that found expression not only in Pharaonic Egypt but also in ancient Greek and Byzantine culture. We will attend, in particular, to Saint Symeon the New Theologian and hesychast tradition.

---

[18] Mikhail Lermontov, "The Angel" (1831), as reproduced in Christopher Bamford's Introduction to Nikolai Berdyaev, *The Russian Idea* (Hudson, New York: Lindisfarne Press, 1992), p. 7. The English-language translator of this poem is not specifically identified.

[19] It has been observed in a psychoanalytic context that reverie "can be visual, olfactory, kinaesthetic, etc., no less than auditory or musical." See Riccardo Lombardi, "Time, Music, and Reverie," *Journal of the American Psychoanalytic Association*, Volume 54, Issue 4, December 1, 2008, pp. 1191-1211. Information on-line at: <https://doi.org/10.1177%2F0003065108326107> (Accessed 1/10/2021)

2. Luminance

God first created light, All men are born out of it.
— Kabir

In Russia, the idea of the author as Prophet—the idea that a writer could be more than a writer, a combination of secular saint, ascetic hero, holy fool and martyr—has been accepted, if not assumed, throughout both the 19th and the 20th Centuries.[20]
— Philip Gorski

Archetypal psychologist, James Hillman (d. 2011) wrote that the imaginal world "is neither literal nor abstract and yet is utterly real, with its own laws and purposes."[21] Theologian and scholar of mythology and depth psychology, Norvene Vest, wrote that "[t]he imaginal is a mode of knowledge based not primarily in the sensory and the empirical, nor primarily in the conceptual and ideational; rather it rests between senses and ideas, in a true realm largely forgotten today."[22] In the imaginal flow with which we are concerned in this book, we may, without disruption to the narrative, shift to another image—the caterpillar, prior to its becoming a butterfly. In this intermediate stage, its

---

[20] Philip Gorski, *Goodseekers: Essays on Literature and Spirituality, East and West* (Sherwood Rise, Nottingham, U.K.: The AlphaOmega Press, 2019), p. 12.
[21] James Hillman, *A Blue Fire: Selected Writings by James Hillman*, edited by T. Moore. (New York: HarperPerennial, 1991), p. 6. For Tom Cheetham, however, the literal and the conceptual are always abstract and literal truth is always false. Cheetham also understands literalism as a kind of madness.
[22] Norvene Vest, "Is Reverie to be Trusted? The Imaginal and the Work of Marija Gimbutas," *Feminist Theology*, 2005, Volume 13, Issue 2, pp. 239-248, p. 239. Preview on-line at: <https://journals.sagepub.com/doi/abs/10.1177/0966735005051950#articleCitationDownloadContainer> (Accessed 10/27/2020)

chrysalis, the caterpillar is undergoing a kind of alchemy on all the elements of its being. We may say that the caterpillar, in its chrysalis, is in a state of reverie, trusting the darkness. This is the darkness within which the luminance appears—the dark luminance that will, in due time, emerge as the brightly colored butterfly—a totally different being than the caterpillar. This is also the image of where we are as a globally inter-connected civilization that is dying. This is no less the state of affairs of any writer or other artist submitting to the creative process.

The concern with reverie, in this present book, is concern with the roots of creativity. While there is no special claim to luminosity in this book, there is a desire to celebrate the possibility that writings by any, or at least some, authors may come to embody and convey the divine light.[23] One such contemporary author who comes to mind is Priest-Monk Silouan of the Wisdom Hermitage at St. Davids, Wales. Hieromonk Silouan is author of a series of wisdom texts as well as shorter writings. The books are *Wisdom Songs* (2011), *Wisdom and Wonder* (2011), *Wisdom, Prophecy and Prayer* (2013), *Wisdom, Glory and the Name* (2014), and *Merlin on Manstone Mynd* (2016). This last title "represents the wisdom themes of [the previous books] ... in story form, through the figure of Merlin living on the Stiperstones, here called Manstone Mynd, in the historical setting of the Sixth Century. It unravels the powerful energies of the quartzite tors and ancient mines in the light of the Song of the Name, brought back from Byzantium by Taliesin the Bard."[24] This last title also contains reflections on the nature of the Holy Grail. The character of Taliesin embodies for Fr. Silouan a kinship between Byzantium and ancient Britain or Albion. As a literary device, the presentation of Taliesin—as well as the whole structure of the book—manifests the luminosity that we are concerned with here.

All writers who experience themselves as having the freedom to decide how and what they will write would be fortunate indeed if they

---

[23] According to Professor Nichifor Tănase (Eftimie Murgu University, Romania), the terms "luminous" (*shaphya*) and "luminosity" (*shaphyutha*) are key terms in the great East Syrian writers on the spiritual life in the seventh and eighth centuries (Ephrem, John of Apamea, and Philoxenus of Mabbugh).
[24] Priest-Monk Silouan, "Wisdom Centuries," at Wisdom Hermitage website. On-line at: <http://www.wisdomhermitage.org.uk/wisdom-songs-2011/> (Accessed 6/2/2020)

recognized this possibility in themselves. Fr. John Dupuche (Catholic Theological College, Melbourne, Australia) writes:

> Just as the image on the surface of the mirror exists already in a certain sense in the mirror, so too the world exists essentially in God. That which exists in time pre-exists somehow in eternity. The infinite Silence which expresses itself completely in the Word takes pleasure also in expressing itself partially in the cosmos. The "I," whose self-consciousness is "I am," expresses itself in "I am this and that," that is, in the objective world. The Word, which is the original revelation, is the foundation of all revelations. It is the truth at the heart of all truths; it is the primordial mantra at the heart of all mantras. This world is the free work, the play of him who is essentially free.[25]

In this present text we will explore the free play of the "I am," the Word, in our circumstances of limitation and mortality. We will look particularly at the human reality as it has been variously imagined in Christian tradition. Within this tradition, the luminance or luminosity associates especially with what are called sacraments or mysteries. As Vlad Naumescu (Central European University, Budapest, Hungary) has pointed out, "Eastern Christianity developed the language of *mysteries* as a form of mediation between the immaterial and material worlds."[26] The divine luminance or luminescence (radiance) is both healing and liberating. This divine luminance is also what is traditionally called the "uncreated light."[27] It is the "light of Christ" that appears at the Easter/Pascha vigil—a light that is "not different" from the Life or

---

[25] John R. Dupuche, "Towards a Christian Tantra: The Interplay of Christianity and Kashmir Shaivism," p. 78. On-line at: <https://repository. divinity.edu.au/1628/1/Towards_a_Christian_Tantra._for_Antoine_Serval-1.pdf> (Accessed 5/31/2020)

[26] Vlad Naumescu, "Learning the 'Science of Feelings': Religious Training in Eastern Christian Monasticism," *Ethnos: Journal of Anthropology*, Volume 77, Number 2, 2012, pp. 227-251. On-line at: <https://www.tandfonline.com/doi/full/10.1080/00141844.2011.595809> (Accessed 7/25/2020)

[27] The uncreated light is discussed further below at Section 9, "Saint Symeon and the Uncreated Light."

Glory of the Holy Trinity. This Light/Glory manifests as the Divine and the Created Sophia, which is the one single Sophia of God.[28]

On a webpage of one particular (Russian Orthodox) church in Russia, there is this expression: "The more temples, the less hospitals and prisons."[29] This expression makes sense only if we understand that not every church manifests as a temple of the Spirit channeling the healing and liberating warmth and light of the divine radiance/luminance.[30] May you be sustained in the awareness that some do exist. The divine radiance/ luminance seems most powerfully at home in certain kinds of poetry. In the words of Jamaican poet, Lorna Goodison, "Good poetry is like effective prayer, it feeds the human spirit, it nourishes, it puts us in touch with forces far greater than ourselves."[31] It has been long known in indigenous cultures that the stories we tell, whether to others or to ourselves, have healing (or destructive) potential.[32] Reverie, as we are considering it in this present

---

[28] See my book, *From Glory to Glory: The Sophianic Vision of Fr. Sergius Bulgakov*. A Perennials Study Group publication, Memphis, Tennessee. (CreateSpace, 2016).

[29] In Russian, the expression is "Чем больше храмов, тем меньше больниц и тюрем." From a webpage of a church in the Mytishchi deanery of the Moscow diocese of the Russian Orthodox Church.

[30] As author and poet, Tom Cheetham, has noted, temples are the archetypal "places" where presence occurs. These are places in opposition to the abstract space and time of modern science, and modern technological life. (*Imaginal Love*, previously cited, p. 152)

[31] As quoted at *The Poetry Archive*, on-line at: <https://poetryarchive.org/poet/lorna-goodison/> (Accessed 8/16/2020)

[32] See the published work of author and psychiatrist, Lewis Mehl-Madrona, including *Healing the Mind through the Power of Story: The Promise of Narrative Psychiatry* (Rochester, Vermont: Bear & Company, 2010) and *Narrative Medicine: The Use of History and Story in the Healing Process* (Rochester, Vermont: Bear & Company, 2007). In his Introduction to Colette Aboulker-Muskat's book, *Mea Culpa: Tales of Resurrection*, Dr. Gerald Epstein says that it was the view of Rabbi Zvi Yehuda Kook (d. 1982), son of the first Ashkenazi chief rabbi of British Mandatory Palestine, that all illness is possession. It is from that perspective that both story and imagery contribute to health maintenance by performing a kind of exorcism or cleansing of the embodied psyche. Reverie is both the entertainment of, and the ingestion of, phenomena.

text, hovers in that "space" between thought and prayer.[33] As an illustration of that space between thought and prayer, here is a poem by Alexander Pushkin, who is considered by many to be the greatest Russian poet. This is an untitled 8-verse poem from 1829 that, in this translation by Peter Bird, is called "Pushkin's 'Reverie'":

While wandering a noisy roadway,
Or entering a crowded church,
Or sitting with the crazy young folk,
I fall into my reverie:

I think again: The years are marching;
The number left we cannot see.
We all must pass the eternal archway,
Each at his hour, inexorably.

When I behold a lonely oak tree,
I think: A forest patriarch;
It will outlive my time and memory,
As grandfather's it also marked.

While cradling a lovely baby,
Immediately I think: farewell!
I yield my place, so yours it may be:
As I fade, your bloom shall swell.

Each day, as days roll on to year-end,
I escort with familiar thoughts:
Which day will be the anniversary
When by slow death I will be caught?

---

[33] See Marilyn Mathew, "Reverie: between thought and prayer," July 2005, *Journal of Analytical Psychology*, Volume 50, Number 3, pp. 383-93. Abstract on-line at: <https://www.researchgate.net/publication/7814997_Reverie_between_thought_and_prayer> (Accessed 9/15/2020). In this paper, "[r]everie as a quality of thought akin to prayer is explored in the relationship between self and other." A fruitful question to ponder: When, or under what conditions, does reverie itself become prayer?

And where will fate my ending tally?
In war, abroad, or on the sea?
Perhaps the very next small valley
My cooling ashes will receive?

Although, in truth, a senseless body
Is careless where it lies, at best,
Yet close to my beloved country
Is where I long to take my rest.

And let this be: By my sepulcher
Young life will come to play, in time.
And let indifferent, thoughtless Nature
Eternally in beauty shine.

As one might expect for language that hovers between thought and prayer, this translation/adaptation can also be sung.[34] There is a saying, "The world seeks to be admired by you!" Consider the myriads of tiny heliotropes that bloom in the sunlight along any roadside. Each one begs for your attention. Each one wants to be noticed! Psychotherapist, Robert D. Romanyshyn (Pacifica Graduate Institute) writes in this way about the rose blossom:

> … I wondered what strange alchemy must transpire in that place which, farthest from the ground of our daily concerns, is the first to receive the warmth of the morning sun and then later the light of the stars and the glow of the moon. In the alchemy of reverie the hard edges of the world are dissolved as things reveal their secrets and announce their dreams. In this place, the witness knows the world in a different way than does the critic, and, taking leave of him, frees the world into its aweful mysteries. On one such occasion, I saw how a rose so fully desired to be itself that it opened beyond its own boundaries, drinking in the light, becoming pure light itself before its pedals would begin to fall away. In that moment, I realized a won-

---

[34] This English translation of Alexander Pushkin's untitled 1829 poem is by Peter Bird who is also a choral composer. Bird's translation/adaptation of this poem can be found on-line at: <http://peterbird.name/choral/Pushkins_Reverie/Pushkins_Reverie.html> (Accessed 11/12/2020)

derful secret of the world: that a rose is a flowering of the sun, the light's way of becoming blossom and seed, odor and color, texture and visibility.[35]

We may offer for reflection the proposal of two images as primal sources of luminance in the Christian world—the Virgin Mary in her iconographic identification as the Burning Bush—the Virgin Mary as the fire that illuminates and warms, but does not consume—and the Virgin Mary as Life-Giving Fountain. Elsewhere in this present book reference is made to the notion of humankind as having a dual origin—from heavenly realms and from Earth. These two sources of human-kind can be associated in imagery (in contemplation) with these two primal images of the Blessed Virgin Mary as together being at the symbolic root of all the luminosity or luminance that we are capable of experiencing—the light of Life. It is within the energetic field between these two, as it were, "magnetic poles" that the imaginal dynamism propels us "outward" in the knowing/unknowing of our life's journey, much as in the madness or the prophetic illumination of Sancho Panza in the foolishness or the nobility of his quest in Cervantes' *Don Quixote*. In the tradition with which we are concerned, both God and His Light are mysteries.

In this section on Luminance we have been concerned with the light or luminosity inherent in all things that, by virtue of their place in the manifest world, retain the life-sustaining link with the divine life. It is part of the thought-world of Jacob Boehme (d. 1624) that all things have their "signature," their "word" that they strain to speak to human-kind. Or we might say that each thing *is* a divine word being spoken to us. Glenn McCullough (Seneca College) writes, "In short, understan-ding grants the ability to perceive all of the archetypes and their 'signatures' in the created order, with an emphasis on the ability to see how they all form a unity in God."[36] Reverie is a listening for, and to, these words. This present book is an exploration of this insight.

---

[35] Robert D. Romanyshyn, "On Angels and Other Anomalies of the Imaginal Life," London, 2003. On-line at: <http://www.robertromanyshyn.com/files/documents/On-Angels-and-Other-Anomalies-of-the-Imaginal-Life.pdf> (Accessed 1/11/2021)

[36] Glenn J. McCullough, "Jacob Boehme and the Spiritual Roots of Psycho-dynamic Psychotherapy: Dreams, Ecstasy, and Wisdom," Ph.D. dissertation, Toronto School of Theology, University of St. Michael's College, 2019, p. 159.

3.   The *Imaginarium* (Oratory)

Ancient observatory, Delhi, India

What was some time ago dubbed (erroneously) "post-modernity" and what I've chosen to call, more to the point, "liquid modernity," is the growing conviction that change is the only permanence, and uncertainty the only certainty. A hundred years ago "to be modern" meant to chase "the final state of perfection"—now it means an infinity of improvement, with no "final state" in sight and none desired.[37]
— Zygmunt Bauman

Fabulation, then, means not a turning away from reality, but an attempt to find more subtle correspondences between the reality which is fiction and the fiction which is reality.[38]
— Robert E. Scholes

The rationale for this section in our narrative has to do, in the first instance, with the correct analysis of our present situation, which can be called either modernity or post-modernity.[39] Either way, the fundamental underlying assumptions, not always made explicit, remain the unchanged. In this time, in the United States, for example, we are living through a "perfect storm" of public health crisis (COVID-19),

---

On-line at: <https://tspace.library.utoronto.ca/handle/1807/99728> (Accessed 2/27/2021)

[37] Zygmunt Bauman, *Liquid Modernity* (Malden, Massachusetts: Polity Press, 2012), Foreword to the 2012 Edition, Kindle location 82.

[38] Robert E. Scholes, *Fabulation and Metafiction* (Urbana, Illinois: University of Illinois Press, 1979), p. 8.

[39] A somewhat different type of analysis, referred to by the term "metamodernism," can be characterized as a post-modernism that situates itself beyond an emphasis on deconstruction.

economic crisis (massive unemployment), and civil unrest due to failures of justice.[40] Beyond that, there is the whole range of systemic failures around the planet including climate change and environmental degradation.

The above quote by the Polish-British sociologist and philosopher, Zygmunt Bauman (d. 2017), underscores the inclination to believe that all these problems can be addressed by making smaller or larger incremental adjustments to present systems or ideologies, not requiring any re-thinking of fundamental assumptions. This will eventually be seen to be a mistake. What is really required of all of us at this time in our history—and indeed in all places and times—is remembrance of who we are, from whence we have come, and to where we are going. Present ills in this world will not be solved by incremental adjustments. Reverie is the gateway to remembrance and conditions that enable reverie enable remembrance.

The quote above by the American literary critic and theorist, Robert Scholes (d. 2016), is meant to highlight the ambiguity of borderlines between reality and the fictional. The nature of this borderline is like a Mobius strip, which is to say the border is always imputed and "after the fact." In terms of the metaphor of the Mobius strip, we do not encounter any border as we move along the strip. What we do encounter is either one thing or the other, but not any explicit border between them. We simply discover that what was, for example, "inner" now appears to us as "outer."[41] Other dualities or binaries could be offered. For example, the duality of "observer" and the "observed" is such that, as the theoretical physicist, David Bohm

---

[40] The situation is made worse because the United States has not, so far, fully formed itself as a single people. It has not received the wisdom of the indigenous peoples of this continent nor has it remembered itself in relation to images of Monsalvat and the Grail. In *The Rose of the World*, a visionary text by Daniil Andreev, Monsalvat is the *zatomis* (top layer) of the metaculture of North-Western Europe, North America, Australia, and some parts of Africa. Metacultures, in Andreev's writing, seem to function as something like templates for the formation of peoples (nations).

[41] *Neurographica* is a contemporary method of creating mind and body connections through a combination of art and psychology. The author of the method is Pavel Piskarev, a Russian/Israeli architect and psychologist. Production of this type of art—and perhaps some other types of art as well— occurs at the interface between conscious effort and the sub-conscious. Neurographic art re-awakens and restores the ability to dream and to envision.

(d. 1992), had noted, these are mutually formative, whether it is phenomena "out there" that are being observed or thoughts or other phenomena "in here" (that is, "inner") that are being observed.[42] We will
have occasion to refer again to David Bohm further below.

> The observatory he had built didn't have any peers in the
> world. It was a three-story, round building, constructed to
> facilitate a connection to the stars. You can read about Ulugh
> Beg's scientific achievements; they were brilliant, but his
> psychological work remains unknown. I told you that the
> people here were big dreamers, that they worked with the sub-
> stance of death and dreams, and that they preserved powerful
> ways of transformation. The work performed here was aimed
> at making immortality available to as many people as possible.[43]
> — Michael, an Uzbek healer

Reality, from within the context of these present reflections on reverie,
can be characterized as that which serves as pole star to our life—that
to which we orient and conform our life.

Macrocosm/mesocosm/microcosm. A controlling metaphor for this present
text is the *observatory*. Observatories in ancient times had a broader
function than they do today. The observatory can be understood as a
"place" for searching deeply through particular selected imaginaries.
The Tower of Babel was most likely an observatory turned toward the
service of the collective ego. The end result could only be its destruction. A central consideration might be the relation between the
human species and the worlds beyond it. This is usually expressed in
some version of the *macrocosm/microcosm* duality. Sometimes it is imaged
as a triad, the terms of which are *macrocosm/mesocosm/microcosm.* In this
triad, the intermediate region or *mesocosm* is also sometimes named the

---

[42] See, for example, Chapter 5, "The Observer and the Observed," in David
Bohm, *On Dialogue*, edited by Lee Nichol (London: Routledge, 1996, 2004).
This was a topic, particularly, in conversations between David Bohm and
Jiddhu Krishnamurti.
[43] In Olga Kharitidi, *Master of Lucid Dreams* (Charlottesville, Virginia: Hampton
Roads Publishing Company, 2001), p. 159. The great observatory of Ulugh
Beg (1394-1449) was located in the Central Asian city of Samarkand, in what
is today southeastern Uzbekistan.

Mundus Imaginalis or imaginal world.[44] These "regions," if we may refer to them in this way, can be understood as relating to each other as "sides" of a Mobius strip. We will have more to say about the *mesocosm* further below but first we will consider the simpler binary, *microcosm/macrocosm*.

Citing Leontius of Jerusalem (485-543), the iconographer, Br. Aidan Hart, writes:

> The material world, as vast as it is quantitatively, is actually contained in the human person; it has its destiny in the human person. We are a *macrocosm*, a large world within a small world. This is the basis of our priestly task. The material world becomes fully articulate through us in the praise of God. We were also created to offer the world in thanksgiving, to be Eucharistic creatures.

> Through heaven and earth and sea, through all creation visible and invisible, I offer veneration to the creator of all things. For it is *through me* that the heavens declare the glory of God, *through me* the moon worships God, through me the stars glorify Him, *through me* the waters and showers of rain, the dew and all creation venerate God and give Him glory. (Leontius of Jerusalem)[45]

What is striking about this perspective is the notion that the human reality is not the *microcosm* but, rather, the *macrocosm*. The cosmos is contained within us. To cite another example of this same perspective, Rumi (1207-1273), according to William Chittick, "remarks that philosophers say that man is the *microcosm*, while theosophers or Sufis say

---

[44] The imaginal world, at least in the understanding of Henry Corbin, is not a world of human creation (or imaginings). Within the imaginal realm the initiative lies within the angelic world. Within the imaginal realm, we (as humans) are being imagined. Instead of the familiar expression of infinite regress, "turtles all the way up (or down)," we might offer this: "It's *angels* all the way up and *angels* all the way down."

[45] Br. Aidan Hart, "Icons and the Material World," an address given at Iona, Scotland, September 28, 2000, p. 3. On-line at: <https://aidanharticons.com/wp-content/uploads/2012/08/ICONSMAT.pdf> (Accessed 6/6/2020). Italics added.

that man is the *macrocosm* ...."[46] It is from within this particular strand of the tradition that we can hope to make sense of the words of the Uzbek healer, Michael, quoted above, about the function of the observatory in Samarkand—a function that has a psychological (or inner) dimension. We play with that notion in this present text as a child might play with a small telescope or looking glass. Which end does one look through? Well, of course, the answer is either—unless one has a particular purpose in looking. The situation is very much like the Byzantine Christian palindrome (in ancient Greek letters) that appears in mosaic tile over the fountain in front of the Great Church of the Hagia Sophia in Istanbul: *Nipson anomēmata mē monan opsin* (meaning: "Wash your sins, not only your face"). Like the macrocosm/microcosm reversibility, the palindrome is also reversible. Its meaning remains the same, whether the letters are read from left to right or from right to left.[47]

Like the palindrome that makes sense in either direction, whether we inquire about a unity within reverie or a unity with ourselves, unity may be discerned and achieved. Otherwise, we are simply daydreaming and allowing ourselves to become dissociated.[48] In the case of ourselves, such unity cannot be assumed and is not assured. When we have awakened from reverie, we might then be able to ask ourselves where the reverie was taking us. Was it taking us toward dissolution or toward some higher synthesis? The alchemical chaos could go in either direction.

When, in the midst of life, we find ourselves in conditions like the demoniac in the Gospel who said, "My name is Legion" (Mark 5:9), we may recognize and respond to the invitation to work on ourselves, which is an exercise of discrimination and will.[49] Gurdjieff wrote:

---

[46] William C. Chittick, *The Sufi Doctrine of Rumi: Illustrated Edition* (Bloomington, Indiana: World Wisdom, 2005), p. 52.

[47] From within our observatory—*imaginarium* (oratory)—this palindromic character applies also to the historical process. History, depending upon our purposes, can be read from within our observatory as either evolutionary or devolutionary. It is also important to remember, as Tom Cheetham writes (*Imaginal Love*, p. 100), citing Henry Corbin, "We are not in history. History is in us."

[48] Dissociation is thought to play a role in schizophrenia and what is called borderline personality disorder.

[49] In Boris Ferapontoff's "Notes from Constantinople," Gurdjieff (and/or P. D. Ouspensky) said something like: "Unity is the psychological attribute of

Man has no permanent and unchangeable I. Every thought, every mood, every desire, every sensation, says "I." And in each case it seems to be taken for granted that this I belongs to the *Whole*, to the whole man, and that a thought, a desire, an aversion is expressed by this Whole. ... Man's every thought and desire appears and lives quite separately and independently of the Whole. And the Whole never expresses itself, for the simple reason that it exists, as such, only physically as a thing, and in the abstract as a concept. Man has no individual I. ... *Man is a plurality.*[50]

Formation of a coherent unitary self—in both the image and the likeness of the divine coherence, which is a *coinherence*—is the task set before us when each of us comes into this world. Reverie, of itself, will not contribute to this *unless* there is something in us that seeks to discern (listens for) the unity behind and within the phenomena—the divine melody—in response to which we may be re-born into new life (the second birth). This melody is the directedness within the imaginal. Writing about psycho-cosmology of Henry Corbin, Tom Cheetham writes:

One crucial element ... is the absolutely central place that music has in his imagination. It is music, the harmony of things, that ties all creation together. In the Beginning the voices of the Angels sang the world into being. The Angel's voice often comes as music. It most often comes only as the fragment of a song that we almost hear, at the edge of the

---

immortality." From Joseph Azize, posted as a blog entry by Sophia Wellbeloved on-line at: <https://gurdjieffbooks.wordpress.com/2008/09/08/unity-is-the-psychological-attribute-of-immortality/> (Accessed 11/2/2020)

[50] P. D. Ouspensky, *In Search of the Miraculous* (New York: Harcourt Brace Jovanovich, 1949), p. 58. Italics are in the original. As quoted in Joseph Azize, "Solar Mysticism in Gurdjieff and Neoplatonism," *Crossroads: An Interdisciplinary Journal for the Study of History, Philosophy, Religion, and Classics,* 2010, Volume 5, Issue 1, pp. 18-26, p. 22. On-line at: <http://www.uq.edu.au/crossroads/Archives/Vol%205/Issue%201%202010/Vol5Iss110%20-%204.Azize%20(p.18-26).pdf> (Accessed 11/11/2020)

world we know, and even the dimmest memory of it can break your heart.[51]

Cheetham writes further about the central place of music in Corbin's account of the imagination:

> The notion of harmony and harmonic resonances among the different worlds in the imaginal realm is a central metaphor in all his work. He draws on Platonic and Neoplatonic notions of harmony and the music of the spheres, which have had such an important role in the theologies of the monotheistic religions and among mystics in every tradition.[52]

This same music or melody is the dynamism of the imaginal, as understood in this present book, and of reverie.[53] This melody is also the song that the poet knew in this poem by Robert Lax:

> there are not many songs
> there is one song
> the animals lope to it
> the fish swim to it
> the sun circles to it
> the stars rise
> the snow falls
> the grass grows
>
> there is no end to the song and no beginning
> the singer may die
> but the song is forever
>
> truth is the name of the song
> and the song is truth.[54]

---

[51] Tom Cheetham, *Imaginal Love*, p. 33.

[52] Tom Cheetham, *Imaginal Love*, p. 175. Cheetham also observed, in the same work (at p. 144) that metaphors are not tropes of poetic thought—they are features of the world.

[53] Melody receives considerable attention in my book, *Taliesin's Harp: A Poetics of the Dvine-Humanity*, especially in connection with discussion of its function in the cosmogony of J. R. R. Tolkien.

St. Maximus the Confessor (c. 580-662), some decades after the death of Leontius, also gives expression to the perspective of the human species as *macrocosm*. The Romanian theologian, Fr. Dumitru Stăniloae (d. 1993) wrote:

Some of the Fathers of the Church have said that man is a *microcosm*, a world which sums up in itself the larger world. Saint Maximus the Confessor remarked that the more correct way would be to consider man as a *macrocosm* because he is called to comprehend the whole world within himself, as one capable of comprehending it without losing himself, for he is distinct from the world. Therefore man effects a unity greater than the world exterior to himself whereas, on the contrary, the world as cosmos, as nature, cannot contain man fully within itself without losing him, that is, without losing in this way the most important reality, that part which more than all others gives reality its meaning. The idea that man is called to become "the world writ large" has a more precise expression, however, in the term *macroanthropos*. The term conveys the fact that in the strict sense the world is called to be humanized entirely, that is, to bear the entire stamp of the human, to become panhuman, making real through that stamp a need that is implicit in the world's own meaning, to become in its entirety a humanized cosmos in a way that the human being is not called to become nor can ever fully become, even at the farthest limit of his attachment to the world where he is completely identified with it, a *cosmosized* man. The destiny of the cosmos is found in man not man's destiny in the cosmos. This is shown, not only by the fact that the cosmos is the object of human consciousness and knowledge and not the reverse, but also by the fact that the entire cosmos serves human existence in a practical way.[55]

---

[54] As reproduced in the Epilogue of Michael N. McGregor, *Pure Act: The Uncommon Life of Robert Lax* (New York: Fordham University Press, 2015), p. 393. The poem can also be found on-line at <https://www.robertlax.com/remembering-robert-lax-on-the-20th-anniversary-of-his-death/> (Accessed 11/16/2020) and elsewhere.

[55] Dumitru Stăniloae, *Orthodox Dogmatic Theology: The Experience of God* (Brookline, Massachusetts: Holy Cross Orthodox Press, 2005), as quoted in a lecture by Fr. Andrew Louth on "Maximus the Confessor and Modern

Teachings of the macrocosm/microscosm were most extensively developed within Jewish Kabbalah. We will not be able to enter into that body of literature and teaching here, but we will simply note that Rabbi Yitzhaq of Acre (14th century), said, "Every human being is a microcosm (*olam qatan*), and the world as a whole is a macro-human being."[56]

To highlight the continuation of the strand of the tradition according to which humankind constitutes the *macrocosm*, not the *microcosm* as commonly assumed, we call attention to St. Nicodemus the Hagiorite (1749-1809), an Athonite monk and one of the compilers of the *Philokalia*. George S. Bebis (Professor Emeritus of Patristics at Holy Cross Orthodox Seminary, Brookline, Massachusetts) wrote as follows:

> St. Nicodemos bases his spiritual counsel on a sound scriptural and patristic anthropology. Following St. Gregory the Theologian and St. Gregory Palamas, he rejects Democritos' declaration that man was created by God as a *microcosm* with the greater world of nature. Rather, he holds that man was created as a *macrocosm*, that is, a greater world within the smaller universe. Even compared with the angels, man is a greater world because he is composed both of the invisible and the visible worlds, whereas the angels are composed only of the invisible world. Immediately, St. Nicodemos describes the human body as a palace and the mind who dwells in it, which shows the balance and correct understanding of both components of human existence, the physical and the spiritual.[57]

Science" via a blog post titled, "The human person as priest of the cosmos," by Macrina Walker at the blog, *A Vow of Conversation*, April 30, 2009. On-line at: <https://avowofconversation.wordpress.com/2009/04/30/the-human-person-as-priest-of-the-cosmos/> (Accessed 6/7/2020). Italics added.

[56] As quoted by Ya'qub ibn Yusuf at his bookshop's webpage for a course on "Reb Nahman's Universe: the Torah of the Void." Elsewhere, Ya'qub ibn Yusuf notes that "… the Tzaddiq is a microcosm in which the macrocosm may be found." From Ya'qub Ibn Yusuf, "The Archetype of the Tzaddiq in Hasidic Tradition," Master's thesis, University of Manitoba, 1992, p. 201. On-line at: <http://mspace.lib.umanitoba.ca/bitstream/1993/18558/1/Ibn_Yusif_The_archetype.pdf> (Accessed 7/27/2020)

[57] George S. Bebis, Introduction to Nicodemos of the Holy Mountain, *A Handbook of Spiritual Counsel*, Classics of Western Spirituality series (Paulist Press, 1988), p. 48.

This *reversed* perspective—that is, reversed from the common point of view—in which the human is the *macrocosm* is elaborated by Richard Smoley in his book, *Inner Christianity*. Here he is writing in a chapter titled "The Mystical Body of Christ":

> … Here it [the Church] is likened to a human body as a whole; each individual is a cell or "member" of this body. The idea goes back to Paul: "For as we have many members in one body, and all members have not the same office; so we being many, are one body in Christ, and every one members of one another" (Romans 12:4-5). Paul was very likely influenced by Jewish esoteric thought, which envisages the whole human race as Adam Kadmon, the primordial man. In Christianity, this idea evolved into the image of the church as the Mystical Body of Christ. …
>
> …
>
> The inner church is a living, organic body. As this passage indicates, evoking Paul, who speaks of the "diversities of gifts, but the same Spirit" (1 Cor. 12:4), each "member" of this body has a different function, like the body's own organs. In this *macrocosmic* human, the Christ consciousness is the animating principle, the life force that unites and coordinates the individual "members," just as a hidden but omnipresent intelligence in ourselves keeps all our cells working in harmony. "There are diversities of operations, but it is the same God which worketh all in all.... For as the body is one, and hath many members, and all the members of that one body, being many: so also is Christ" (1 Cor. 12:6, 12-13).
>
> This idea can be found in many corners of the Christian tradition—for example, in Renaissance Kabbalists such as Pico della Mirandola and Cornelius Agrippa—but the Christian esotericist who takes this idea the furthest is Emanuel Swedenborg, who says, "Heaven in its totality reflects a single person, and ... it is a person in image and is therefore called the universal human.... For this reason, the heavenly communities that make up heaven are arranged like the members, organs, and viscera in a human being."
>
> Swedenborg takes up another ancient thread of the tradition, beginning with Paul (1 Cor. 12:21-31) …, that each cell or "member" in this body is differentiated in function. The

angels in heaven (all of whom, Swedenborg says, once lived as humans on earth) take their places in this organism on the basis of their dispositions and capacities. Those who are in the head "are supremely involved in everything good." Those in the chest are "involved in the qualities of thoughtfulness and faith"; "people who are in the eyes are in understanding." Those in the ears excel in "attentiveness and obedience," while those in the kidneys, liver, and spleen are occupied with discrimination and purification.

This relentless anthropomorphism may seem quaint, but similar correspondences could be drawn between the body and human society. Each has sectors devoted to producing and circulating nourishment; to protecting from outside attack; to healing and recuperation from damage; to thought and creativity; and to governing and regulating the entity as a whole. Traditional societies often assigned roles in this social organism by heredity or caste, as in the ancient Hindu Laws of Manu. In a freer society it becomes the individual's task to find his own place and serve in the way best suited to his abilities.[58]

In this section we are briefly noting the long history of that strand of tradition concerning the human being that we might call the "high view"—the understanding of the human being as *macrocosm*.[59] We hinted at another (triadic) view consisting of *macrocosm/mesocosm/*

---

[58] Richard S. Smoley, *Inner Christianity: A Guide to the Esoteric Tradition* (Boston, Massachusetts: Shambhala Publications, 2002). As reproduced, without pagination, on-line at: <https://archive.org/stream/InnerChristianityByRichard Smoley/Inner%20Christianity%20by%20Richard%20Smoley_djvu.txt> (Accessed 6/7/2020)

[59] Related to this view of the human as *macrocosm*, but not identical to it, is the ancient notion of the human as having a "divine double" or twin. This little understood view is discussed at length in Charles M. Stang's book, *Our Divine Double* (Cambridge, Massachusetts: Harvard University Press, 2016). See also, Martin Shaw, *Courting the Wild Twin* (White River Junction, Vermont: Chelsea Green Publishing, 2020). The publisher writes: "There is an old legend that says we each have a wild, curious twin that was thrown out the window the night we were born, taking much of our vitality with them. If there was something we were meant to do with our few, brief years on Earth, we can be sure that the wild twin is holding the key." Shaw writes in his book that, for Garcia Lorca, it is *duende* that evokes the wild twin.

microcosm and that the *mesocosm* is also sometimes named, as we said above, the *Mundus Imaginalis* or imaginal world. It is within the imaginal world that our soul is formed. In the Old Testament there is the story of Jacob wrestling with the angel, following which Jacob falls asleep with his head resting on a stone and has a vision of a ladder reaching to heaven, upon which angels are seen ascending and descending. It is this image of a ladder with ascending and descending angels that we may take as emblematic of the character and reality of the *Mundus Imaginalis*. In classical Christian understanding, the soul is that within us which manifests as will, emotion, and desire.[60] The imaginal realm is constituted in such a way as to evoke these manifestations from within us. The imaginal realm is the scene or stage set where the human drama—the drama of soul-making—occurs.[61] The imaginal is distinguished from the imaginary in the following way. In the imaginal realm the object of attention speaks—has something to say. Unlike the merely imaginary, in the imaginal realm the object (or person) speaks back when addressed. It has something to say. It is over-full of meaning that is being communicated to you. When you find yourself discerning patterns or other forms of meaningfulness, you may be confident that the imaginal is being manifested to you.[62] When considered

---

[60] Sometimes this triad is expressed in other terms.

[61] Recall the title of John G. Bennett's multi-volume work, *The Dramatic Universe*, about which Anthony Blake wrote: "The drama is primary. Questions of mechanism and purpose—which still dominate philosophical discourse—are secondary and miss the essential element." In this work the central drama has to do with "the War with Time" (the "merciless heropass"). The perspective in this work, according to Blake, is that "man is made for self-transformation and that this transformation is not predetermined but hazardous. If this is how it is for man, then nothing less can be accepted than that the whole world is hazardous and existence itself is capable of transformation." Blake's commentary can be found on-line at: <https://www.jgbennett.org/the-dramatic-universe-commentary-by-a-g-e-blake/> (Accessed 6/8/2020)

[62] In her book, *Eye of the Heart: A Spiritual Journey into the Imaginal Realm* (Boston, Massachusetts: Shambhala, 2020), Cynthia Bourgeault suggests that *chiasm* seems to be a key pattern in the manifestation of the imaginal. John Moriarty, in his book, *Dreamtime* (Dublin, Ireland: The Lilliput Press, 2020), pointed to this pattern as the Triduum Sacrum, the center and fulcrum of the Christian imaginal. He writes: "Watching him [Jesus], we know there is Palm Sunday before the Triduum Sacrum and Palm Sunday after it. On the Palm

further, you may be left with a sense or realization that you are a character in a dramatic narrative that you do not yet fully understand. To understand this dramatic narrative and your place in it is the Grail quest.

> Because it is not I who look
> But I who am being looked through,
> Gloria.[63]
> — R. S. Thomas

This is the nature of the imaginal realm. It is active and it "sees through" us. "Our" observatory is bi-directional. It is the place of "judgment"—our own—to which we are subject. Another of its names is "conscience." This is the actual place of the (bardo-state) "toll-houses" known in some Orthodox Christian iconography.

Another way of conceiving the *mesocosm* is to see it as a *mandorla*, the "place" where the (any) other two realms overlap. In this conception, the human entity is the *mesocosm* or the meeting place (or crossing) of all worlds or conditions that can be thought of as dualities—heaven and earth, for example, or the paradisal and the abyssal, or the fullness and the void. If we think of this *mandorla* three-dimensionally, we might then conceive of the human as the meeting place of the four elements—earth, air, fire, and water. This "meeting place" then appears as an alchemical retort or a cauldron of transformations. This is functionally similar to the two-dimensional *mandalas* of the various Tantric traditions, these *mandalas* having four sides. The *mandalic* figure can also be found in Christian tradition, in the work of Hugh of St. Victor and others. We will have more to say about *mandalas* further below in the sub-section titled, "Vedanta, Tantra, and Direct Path." Think of these several ways of conceiving the human reality as lenses through which we may observe, from different perspectives, the *energetics* of the human reality. In this book, this is our present task.

In the excerpt above from Richard Smoley, he makes reference to Adam Kadmon, the primordial man, in Jewish mystical tradition. We

---

Sunday after it, the writings of Christian and others mystics are the palms we wave welcoming him back into Christianity." (p. 39)

[63] From the section entitled "Gloria" in a multi-part poem, "Mass for Hard Times," in R. S. Thomas, *Collected Later Poems 1988-2000* (Tarset, U.K.: Bloodaxe Books, 2013), p. 135.

might also call attention to the high view of humankind within Christian tradition as expressed in the writing of Saint Maximus the Confessor (d. 662). Saint Maximus writes about how the world is said to be a man, and in what manner the man is a world, as he heard it told by an unidentified sage:

> And again using a well-known image, he submitted that the whole world, made up of visible and invisible things, is man and conversely that man made up of body and soul is a world. He asserted, indeed, that intelligible things display the meaning of the soul as the soul does that of intelligible things, and that sensible things display the place of the body as the body does that of sensible things. And, he continued, intelligible things are the soul of sensible things, and sensible things are the body of intelligible things; that as the soul is in the body so is the intelligible in the world of sense, that the sensible is sustained by the intelligible as the body is sustained by the soul; that both make up one world as body and soul make up one man, neither of these elements jointed to the other in unity denies or displaces the other according to the law of the one who has bound them together. In conformity with this law there is engendered the principle of the unifying force which does not permit that the substantial identity uniting these things be ignored because of their difference in nature, nor that their particular characteristics which limit each of these things itself appear more pronounced because of their separation and division than the kinship in love mystically inspired in them for union. It is by this kinship that the universal and unique mode of the invisible and unknowable presence in all things of the cause which holds all things together by his existence in all things renders them unmixed and undivided in themselves and in relation to each other. And it shows that they exist by the relationship which unites them to each other rather than to themselves, until such time as pleases the one who bound them together to separate them in view of a greater and more mystical arrangement in the time of the expected universal consummation, when the world, as man, will die to its life of appearances and rise again renewed of it oldness in the resurrection expected presently. At this time the man who is ourselves will rise with the world as a part with the whole and the small with the large, having obtained

the power of not being subject to further corruption. Then the body will become like the soul and sensible things like intelligible things in dignity and glory, for the unique divine power will manifest itself in all things in a vivid and active presence proportioned to each one, and will by itself preserve unbroken for endless ages the bond of unity.[64]

In this vision of the worlds, we see overlapping and inter-penetrating worlds—a relationship, as we noted above, that is named by the word, *mandorla.*

<u>We are not without guidance.</u> Seen from certain points of view, we have no fixed and immovable place to stand—no Archimedean fulcrum, in the classic understanding of this image—as a commonly shared heritage of the wider societies in which we happen to live. This does not mean, however, that we are left without guidance. No people are left without guidance. The question, "What is the nature of this guidance?," is a central and pervasive one that we explore throughout this book. Within Inayati Sufism there is the expression, "Spirit of Guidance," that is a reference to the divine and eternally present emanation of intuition, inspiration, vision, revelation, and prophecy in ways that are accessible to all beings, whatever their level of development, in Planet Earth. The immediate source of this guidance is insight into the implicate order, to use a concept appearing in the work of David Bohm.

Within Sufism, knowledge of the implicate order (the non-manifest) is revealed or perceived through or within the practice of *sama.*[65] This knowledge, however, in the understanding of the Sufi

---

[64] From Chapter Seven of "The Church's Mystagogy," in *Maximus Confessor: Selected Writings*, translated by George C. Berthold, with Introduction by Jaroslav Pelikan, and Preface by Irénée-Henri Dalmais, O.P. (Mahwah, New Jersey: Paulist Press, 1985), pp. 196-197. For an entrance into the best of contemporary Maximus scholarship, see the work of Fr. Doru Costache, Senior Lecturer in Patristic Studies, Saint Cyril's Coptic Orthodox Theological College, Sydney, Australia.

[65] *Sama* is closely connected with the practice of *zikr. Sama* means "listening" while *zikr* means "remembrance." The practice of *sama* may include singing, playing instruments, dancing, recitation of poetry and prayers, and symbolic gestures.

43

teacher Ibn 'Arabi (d. 1240), is normally reserved for the saints—Ibn 'Arabi is regarded by some as Seal of the Saints—but especially to such figures as al-Khidr, the Verdant One.[66] There is in Sufi literature a story of Moses and Khidr. In this story Moses asks to travel with Khidr and he is given conditional permission—the condition being that Moses not question the actions of Khidr. Moses consents, but finds himself unable to refrain from questioning some of Khidr's actions. The reason Moses is unable to be patient and silent is that Khidr's actions are paradoxical in nature, yet Moses seeks to understand them by means of rational thought. Rational thought, however, is an inadequate means of comprehending events or actions that are paradoxical in nature. If it is true that no one can know realities or manifestations as God himself knows them, this is why Christian scripture admonishes us not to make judgements. This does not mean, however, that we are without guidance or that we are unable to exercise discernment. It is the nature of divine guidance to progressively come to see all things as God sees them. Divine guidance has the effect of moving our awareness to a larger context. This is also connected with the endless pursuit (or, more accurately, the timeless appeal) of Beauty that is one with Truth and Goodness.

There is a notion of broken symmetries as having something to do with beauty. Nature is replete with broken symmetries. Attention to these broken symmetries in nature sometimes gives way to realization that the apparently broken symmetries are harmonized or resolved in some larger, more comprehensive, symmetries. This is what happens in reverie. In the Platonic aesthetics of ancient Greece the broken symmetries led the mind to find resolution in the unbroken symmetries of the forms. The perfection of manifest or incarnate Beauty required (or unveiled) connection with the transcendent.

Dreams are not stories. They are more like story fragments, half-remembered, crying out for interpretation. Their uncanniness comes from their fragmentary nature—they seem as if they are part of some story, the larger part of which we seem to have forgotten or cannot

---

[66] See the undated paper in development by Kyle J. Shuebrook, "Science and Sufism: A Discussion of David Bohm and Ibn al-'Arabi," at Academia.edu. On-line at: <https://www.academia.edu/2272891/Science_and_Sufism_ A_Discussion_of_David_Bohm_and_Ibn_al_Arabi> (Accessed 8/10/2020)

make out.[67]   A dream told as a coherent story is, therefore, already interpretation. The Spirit of Guidance becomes accessible to us when we, like ancient seers, peer into the "cauldron of dream."[68] In Christian tradition, Holy Scripture is referred to as the Oracles of God.[69]   The primordial cauldron of dream contains all the images and vignettes of Holy Scripture and much more. The "much more" includes the natural worlds and the cultural worlds—the roots of trees as well as the roots of language. In the parlance of economic theory, "black swans" are events that come upon us that, in hindsight, we might have anticipated and yet we did not. The people of Noah's day might have anticipated a cleansing event of some kind, such as the Flood was—but they did not. Consider what happens when a pilgrim visits a holy site, such as any one of the many ruined abbeys scattered across the British Isles. If the pilgrim is of a certain disposition, she or he may experience the ruins as stimulating or evoking reverie. That which is missing or has been lost in the ruins with their broken symmetries—evokes an imaginative response—an imagining or envisioning of what may yet come to be. This is reverie.

---

[67] A dream leaves us unsatisfied until we have discerned its (imputed) "object"—that which enables its coherence. Without that implied object, we would not be able to "tell" our dream in any meaningful way. The same observations may apply to reverie. Insubstantial though it may be, it is that which, within our reverie, is "calling us" toward our true end or *telos* as human beings.

[68] The grail is sometimes referred to as font or "cauldron of story," perhaps because story fragments (in endless supply) lend themselves readily to improvisation and midrash. Midrash of scriptural story fragments or vignettes also finds dramatic expression in what is called bibliodrama. We always need to ask ourselves: What kind of stories are we telling ourselves and each other?

[69] In mystical tradition, Holy Scripture is not so much regarded as a code to be deciphered as a field of infinite meanings. At some deep level, hermeneutics, as art and science of the interpretation of scripture, is akin to the interpret- tation of dream in that it requires similar skill and sensitivity to the layered and fragmentary character of the matter as presented. It also makes use of the notion of real symbols as opposed to conventional signs. Classicist Peter Kingsley writes, "In the old days the best interpreters... knew that the greatest part of interpretation was not to interfere but simply to watch, and listen, and allow the things observed to reveal their meaning." (Peter Kingsley, *In the Dark Places of Wisdom*, Point Reyes, California: Golden Sufi Center Publishing, 1999, p. 51)

<u>The oratory as place of discernment.</u> The word *"imaginarium"* that heads this section of our narrative means simply a "place" for imagination or—more accurately, in this instance—a place for observing the appearances or "imaginaries" that reveal to us, in the largest possible context, the *energetics* of the human condition. Human imagination is distinct from, but continuous with, divine imagination. Ancient observatories can be regarded as *imaginaria*. The observatory at Samarkand was a late example of this type of construction intended for use in this way. The crystal ball or the glass sphere (*orbuculum*) is another, smaller, type of object that has, since ancient times, also served as an *imaginarium*. The art or process of "seeing" in, or from within, these "places" is known as "scrying."[70] Within hesychast Christian tradition, the commonly used term is *constatation*, which means *diakrisis*, discernment or discrimination. It also means perception without pre-judgment.[71] The function of the oratory or *imaginarium* as place of discernment ought to be understood in close relation to another ancient method of discernment, the practice of incubation.[72] This practice, at the root of Western culture, is an entry into reverie in a passive mode. As we note below, in Section 5 ("Trees and the Green Man"), shamanic "travel" can be regarded as reverie in an active mode.[73] The entry into incubation (relative states of sensory deprivation and psychic isolation) enables conditions of primal reverie. To speak of the primal reverie, however, is to speak of the sub-

---

[70] See Angela Voss's paper on the subject titled, "Scrying," published as Chapter 58 in Christopher Partridge, editor, *The Occult World* (New York: Routledge, 2015, 2016). On-line at: <https://mythcosmologysacred.com/wp-content/uploads/2020/08/Scrying.pdf> (Accessed 8/27/2020)

[71] See Robin Amis, *A Different Christianity: Early Christian Esotericism and Modern Thought* (Albany, New York: State University of New York Press, 1995) for extensive reference to the term, *constatation*, especially as it is used in the *Gnosis* trilogy by Boris Mouravieff.

[72] The practice of iatromantic incubation has been discussed extensively by Peter Kingsley in his book, *In the Dark Places of Wisdom*, previously cited, and in his other writings. Another resource for this practice is Carl. A. Meier, *Healing Dream and Ritual: Ancient Incubation and Modern Psychotherapy*, 4th edition (Einsiedeln, Switzerland: Daimon Verlag, 2009). The practice of "going down" in incubation also associates with symbolics of grottoes and holy wells in Marian spirituality.

[73] It is an open question whether reverie is usually or typically experienced in a passive mode. I believe that it is.

representational and the sub-propositional.[74] It is from within these conditions that religions and metaphysics—all sacred arts—have their roots and come to birth.

Within this tradition, the human person (oneself) is the "place" from which, and into which, we peer deeply—to understand (to *see*) ourselves, our condition, as we truly are. The human being is (or contains) a vastness! We are, in other terms, the *oratory* or *hesychas-terion*—the "place" of prayer.[75] This is made especially clear in acknowledgment of the human as *macrocosm*. Heaven communicates with Earth in diverse ways. *Symbology* is one of these ways. It is not simply a matter of single isolated symbols—it is, rather, the experience of tissues or interconnected layers of symbols. It is communication as if in a dream.

Imaginaries provide the necessary backdrop or background for our readings of "the present." Consider what value there may be in the current state of affairs (in this time of "the virus") in the world. Chaos *can* be understood as a time when something is birthing, coming to birth. In this, we are moving from one "imaginary" to another. This is similar to becoming multi-lingual. The risk, of course, is that our personal and collective transformations will fail to be realized. The present era—since creation of nuclear power and use of the nuclear bomb—has come to an end. Whether recognized or not, the era has come to an end with the appearance of "the virus" around the globe.

When we look deeply into our *imaginarium*, our object of reverie, the human person, what may we discern? We may discern that the human person as coincidence of opposites—as God is coincidence of opposites. We may also discern the imaginal roots of logic. The common logic is based on the assumption that the world or reality is "logical"—self-consistent—which it is not. All logics are fundamentally "dream logic." This is not to say, however, that logics are not useful in their delimited contexts. There is progressive revelation of the divine order, but this has tended to be papered over by the Hellenic

---

[74] The psychologist, John Vervaeke, has referred to the sub-representational and the sub-propositional in recorded conversation with the psychotherapist, Mark Vernon.

[75] In the words of Robert Sardello, "Prayerfulness is a synonym for Wholeness and even for consciousness," understood in a certain way. From on-line blog entry at: <http://www.robertsardello.com/blog/releasing-the-habit-of-virus-consciousness> (Accessed 7/7/2020)

heritage as we in the modern world have received it. The Hellenic heritage is, however, in reality—in its deep roots—an illuminist heritage. In our *imaginarium*, we may discern, among many other things, Babylon and Zion—transcendent realities that also manifest in the world as we "tune in" to them. We will have more to say about Babylon and Zion further below in Section 7 ("Rastafari as Imagined").

Illuminations/discernments. When we look up and out from the observatory, what do we perceive? We remember that the poet, William Blake (d. 1827), when he looked upward, perceived the all the heavenly hosts, as opposed to seeing the sun as merely a ball of light.[76] Among the further recognitions that might occur to us, in a state of reverie before the God-Man Christ is that, as noted above, even as God is the "place" of paradox, where opposites coincide, so also humankind is the "place" where opposites coincide. The meaning of "freedom" is that there is no "logic" that constrains us in responding to the divine initiative, wherever and whenever that initiative may be discerned. As we sit before the God-Man, the epitome of beauty, it may be that not only discernments arise, but also questions such as, for example, the question of how we might re-pay "the cost of our arising."[77]

Also, as we stand in our *imaginarium* (oratory/observatory) in a state of reverie allowing the focus to widen to its maximum comprehension, we may behold the divine light, the Glory, pervading all things.[78] When the waters are still, we may discern not only "what is" but also "what may be." Knowledge and contemplation of the possibilities of our

---

[76] Psychotherapist, Mark Vernon, in a video conversation with John Vervaeke has noted this characteristic of William Blake.

[77] The expression "cost of our arising" is an allusion to the fourth "obligolnian striving" mentioned by Gurdjieff in his book, *Beelzebub's Tales to His Grandson: All and Everything, First Series* (New York: Penguin Compass, 1999): "The striving from the beginning of their existence to pay for their arising and their individuality as quickly possible, in order afterwards to be free to lighten as much as possible the Sorrow of our Common Father." (Chapter 27, pp. 386).

[78] Within Inayati Sufism there is an understanding of the all-pervasive divine light as constitutive of the very being of humankind. The human journey is to become what we fundamentally already are. See Chapter 4, "Becoming a Being of Light," in Pir Vilayat Inayat Khan, *Awakening: A Sufi Experience* (New York: Jeremy P. Tarcher / Putnam, 1999).

situation is a godlike function of reverie.[79] The Glory (Holy Sophia) is the world and the Life (*Zoe*) of the Holy Trinity. The Glory is both "uncreated" and "created." We are unable to distinguish between these. Because the Glory is all-pervasive, we are unable to say whether we behold it with our "inner eyes" (only) or with our physical eyes (only). Inner and outer are experienced, in this case, as relating to one another as the "sides" of a Mobius strip. "Inner" and "outer" are understood to be in relationship and, ultimately, "not different." Rowan Williams notes the fluidity in our ways of speaking about contemplative experience: "Whether this is called darkness or light, void or plenitude, will depend upon all kinds of contingent factors— traditions of religious rhetoric, exegetical interests, even tem- perament."[80]

The embodied human person as subject as well as object of reverie is reflected, for example, in a substantial and profoundly meditative text by contemporary Orthodox Christian lay theologian, Annick de Souzenelle. The text, in English-language edition, is titled *The Body and its Symbolism*. At the beginning of her Chapter 1 she quotes the Emerald Tablet: "That which is above resembles that which is below, and that which is below resembles that which is above, to accomplish the miracles of one thing." About this classic Hermetic saying, de Souzenelle writes:

> Hermes Trismegistus—the Thrice-Greatest—seals a golden key
> in the Emerald Tablet. With this key, we will attempt to unlock
> the mystery of what appears essential to us as human beings, a
> mystery we are drawn to even when we do not attempt to grasp

[79] Some accounts of divine omniscience suggest that while God knows both possibilities and actualities (including human dispositions and inclinations), God does not know in advance what free choices will be made within the created order, until those choices have been made. God then responds to those choices and mitigates any ill effects resulting from those choices to restore harmony. In the legendarium of J. R. R. Tolkien the divine omniscience is revealed in the Music of the Ainur that adapts to the chaotic dissonance to sound a new theme that is both "like and yet unlike" the previous theme. See "Music of the Ainur" at the Tolkien Gateway, on-line at: <http://tolkiengateway.net/wiki/Music_of_the_Ainur> (Accessed 12/27/2020)

[80] Rowan Williams, *The Way of St. Benedict* (New York: Bloomsbury Con- tinuum, 2020), p. 123.

it, a mystery compelling us and, at the same time, eluding our powerless intellects.

[…]

Hermetic wisdom also says: "Know yourself, and you will know the universe and the gods." This second key invites us to regard *man within the world and the world within man as two sides of the same coin*, the same hidden reality. What joins them is their inner core.

In this respect, the within and the without are foreign to any special concept; they are just links to an "outer layer," the "skin," as in a fruit the skin covers the pulp, which leads to the kernel. Many can only apprehend his individual pulp and kernel by accessing other plans of reality without, however, leaving the realm of his familiar surroundings. Otherwise the philosopher could well ask, as he has in the past, whether the world does not begin and end at the level of the skin … and he will stray into the land of absurdity.[81]

So we might further say that what we are about in this present text concerned with reverie is a kind of kabbalah—a kabbalah of the embodied human person whose reality is a lens designed to refract the uncreated light of "that world" into the many colors of "this world." From this perspective, the uncreated light is an affirmation of the senses.

What else do we discern/observe when we peer into the depths from our observatory/oratory? We may discern, or find ourselves entering, a third world somehow between "that world" (of the One) and "this world" (of the many). Classicist Peter Kingsley has referred to this as the primordial world of our roots—the primordial being the realm between the eternal and this world.[82] For Kingsley, the primordial is that world that is the subject of mythical history and from

---

[81] Annick de Souzenelle, *The Body and its Symbolism: A Kabbalistic Approach*, translated from the French by Christopher Chaplin and Tony James (Wheaton, Illinois: Quest Books / Theosophical Publishing House, 2015), pp. 1-2. Emphasis added.

[82] In Peter Kingsley's podcast conversation with Adyashanti and elsewhere. Adyashanti's *Being Unlimited* podcast, June 25, 2020, on-line at: <https://beingunlimited.org/being-rooted-in-the-eternal-with-peter-kingsley> (Accessed 8/12/2020)

which mythical history arises. It is the history behind the rationalist interpretations. It is the sacred ground of all being.

In the words of Thomas Matus (New Camaldoli Hermitage, Big Sur), "Christian revelation is also rooted in the symbolic language of the human psyche. Christianity is not only, not even primarily, a system of dogmas or conceptualized expressions of faith; it is a universal story, a ritual whose efficacious signs speak to more than just my intellect. Above all it is a personal ideal, an image of what I can and must be."[83] Here are some practical discernments from a contemporary Christian community in Italy:

- Life is a spiritual journey and every person is at a different stage of this extraordinary journey to Awareness.

- We respect others and their ideas so as to be able to discuss constructively and work together to assist poor and marginalized people.

- Accept others as equals by respecting all without distinction.

- We are free to pray with anyone of any religion.

- If one really wants to make a distinction between people, then distinguish between those who exercise kindness, honesty and charity, and those who unfortunately do not.

- Willingness to accept the "different" is one of the loftier goals in the process of human growth and social development. Our notions of "chosen people" are expanded to include the whole of humanity.

- We strive to practice non-violence and forgiveness and to cultivate the ability to love, as Jesus taught—to express love by loving despite everything.

- A great sin may be all the good we could have done but we did not. Another great sin is willful ignorance which, combined with fanaticism, can even kill.

- Spirituality begins with the ability to amend oneself in the small things so as to be able to achieve the greater goals. Who is faithful in a very little is faithful also in much.

---

[83] Thomas Matus, *Yoga and the Jesus Prayer* (Winchester, U.K.: John Hunt Publishing / O Books, 2010), pp. 16-17.

- We support sustainable development that safeguards the natural resources of our planet. Our fellow creatures, the animals, are treated with the respect due to every living being.
- We pray as Jesus taught to us: Our Father who art in heaven… forgive us our debts, as we forgive our debtors… and deliver us from evil.
- God is still speaking… today, right to you, the reader![84]

By means of terms like "macrocosm" and "microcosm" we are not, however, proposing some kind of map of human consciousness. These are simply images.[85]

In this section we have been considering the on-going process of discernment that is part of embodied life. Discernment occurs in contexts of unknowingness. We go through life not knowing and, because this is so, we attempt to discern truth. Pervasive unknowing—of being unable to "see" the possibilities for growth inherent in our situation—is also a liminal condition, a state of transition, a betweenness. In these states of transition, our feet cannot find solid ground. In the following section we reflect on our experience of liminality, a condition that often proves to be generative for reverie. We note, however, that written language can be experienced, for writers and readers alike, as liminal because, in the world of manifestation, there is inevitably a "distance" between what is meant and what is said. Hieroglyphic showings of the divine world, however, are not subject to this distance.

---

[84] This is a simplified restatement of language appearing at the website of *Anima Universale*, a new religious movement and Christian community associated with the spiritual teacher, Swami Roberto (Roberto Casarin). The language at their website is a distillation of their understanding of what it means to be Christian. On-line at: <https://www.animauniversale.org/introduction> (Accessed 9/5/2020). For more about this community, see Massimo Introvigne, "Between 'Essence Religion' and 'Godly Religion': The Italian Communal Esotericism of the Universal Soul Movement," a paper presented at the North American Conference on Esotericism, Michigan State University, Kellogg Center, June 3-6, 2004, and published on-line at *CESNUR: Center for Studies on New Religions*. On-line at: <https://www.cesnur.org/2004/mi_essence.htm> (Accessed 9/5/2020)

[85] Peter Kingsley has pointed out, in conversation with Adyashanti, that Jung did not map the psyche and that it would be hubris to attempt such a thing.

4. Liminal Conditions

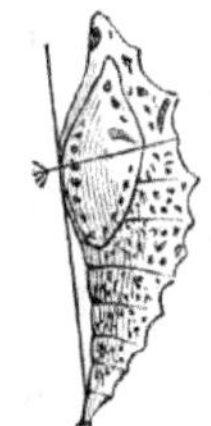

Butterfly chrysalis

> The liminal or in-between space opened by reverie asks us to adopt a religious attitude—one of humility, wonder and awe.[86]
> — Mark Gundry

The feeling-tone of reverie (the "place" of the coincidence of opposites) is one of bitter-sweetness. It is the mixed feeling of the newborn child undergoing both grief at having left the glory of the unborn state and the wonder of breath and of the light of day. It is the feeling of having seen the Holy Grail, but now being unable to find it. It is feeling of having experienced love but, having lost it, only then realizing its worth. Bitter-sweetness seems characteristic of some liminal conditions—conditions in which there may be dawning discernment of a joy on the far side of adversity, suffering, and loss. Consider, for example, the journey known to Native Americans as the "Trail of Tears" as an object of sorrowful reverie. It is an image of the liminal state to be leaving home for destinations and fates unknown. It is not for me to say whether those who walked that trail of leaving home nevertheless experienced moments of joy in the midst of the tragedy but, if they did, then this is the bitter sweetness that (breaks) open hearts. We may hope, for ourselves, nothing less than this. Consider these words of the German poet, philosopher, and phenomenologist of consciousness, Jean Gebser (d. 1973): "The adage that 'how we shout into the woods is how the echo will sound' is undoubtedly true—and the woods are the world. *Everything that happens to us, then, is only the*

---

[86] Mark Gundry in Dana Blue and Caron Harrang, editors, *From Reverie to Interpretation: Transforming Thought into the Action of Psychoanalysis*, first edition (London, United Kingdom: Routledge, 2016), p. 66. Mark Gundry is a psychotherapist in Portland, Oregon.

answer and echo of what and how we ourselves are. And the answer will be an integral answer only if we have approached the integral in ourselves."[87]

The feeling-tone of bitter-sweetness certainly characterizes, for example, the anonymously written Anglo-Saxon poem or lament, "The Wanderer," in Old English.[88] The poem itself *is* reverie—it is *reveriesial* in its production. One might also say that it is, in essence, prayer. It is suggested elsewhere in this present text that reverie hovers between thought and prayer—but reverie may also, as in this lament, manifest itself *as* prayer. If in Christian monastic tradition concerning the practice of meditation it is sometimes suggested that there must be, in the words of Francis Leneghan, a "harnessing of meandering thoughts prior to approaching the stillness of prayer," it is also the case that thoughts, as reverie, may sometimes flow out of that prayerful stillness as expressions of that stillness.[89] It is also evident that the author of this lament was in a liminal state at the time the poem was composed.

At this point, one might wonder about the metaphysics or cosmology that enables or makes possible this exercise of the *imaginarium* that we have been discussing.[90] It has, I believe, something to do with our experience of what is called the liminal, or liminal states. Liminality is about life on the edge, where many of us are living in these times. Another word for this edge is "verge" or borderland. It is the condition of marginality. It is the place of initiation.[91] It is the condition of the caterpillar in its chrysalis prior to its unanticipated rebirth as a

---

[87] Jean Gebser, *The Ever-Present Origin,* translated by Noel Barstad with Algis Mickunas (Athens, Ohio: Ohio University Press, 1986), p. 141. The italics appear in the source text. For an excellent introduction to the work of Gebser, see Jeremy D. Johnson, *Seeing Through the World: Jean Gebser and Integral Consciousness* (Seattle, Washington: Revelore Press, 2019).

[88] An accessible translation of the poem by Jeffrey Hopkins can be found on-line at: <https://www.vqronline.org/essay/wanderer-anglo-saxon-poem-translated-jeffrey-hopkins> (Accessed 2/27/2021)

[89] Concerning this poem, see Francis Leneghan, "Preparing the Mind for Prayer: *The Wanderer, hesychasm* and *theosis*," *Neophilologus,* 2015. On-line at: <https://link.springer.com/article/10.1007%2Fs11061-015-9455-3> (Accessed 2/27/2021)

[90] Of particular relevance is Jeffrey J. Kripal's book, *The Flip: Epiphanies of Mind and the Future of Knowledge* (New York: Bellevue Literary Press, 2019).

[91] In Christian social context, baptism in the early church was an initiation requiring much preparation. In modern times, baptism has become less of an initiatory experience, in the true sense.

butterfly. Liminality is also a state of transition in which a bridge (*barzakh*) to another place, another condition, is appearing under our feet as we walk—one step at a time. The story of the Prodigal Son shows us, however, that it is at the extremities that revelation is given. Poverty is a liminal condition. Sickness is a liminal condition. It is life lived "close to the ground." Liminality is a reference to all the circumstances of life that can be considered tragic.[92] "I create light and I create darkness, I create joy and I create grief, I am YHWH, who do all these things."[93] Salman Bashier (independent scholar of Islamic mysticism and philosophy) has suggested that God, as the Real, is the liminal entity who brings together aspects of non-manifestation and manifesttation.[94]

Consider the life of Jesus. His life was, in so many ways, liminal and yet a psychoanalytics of Jesus reveals no "shadow side."[95] His life manifests a blissfulness that is not ecstatic. This reflects an understanding in the Gospel accounts that the Jesus's conception was not a

---

[92] The tragic dimension of life is not unrelated to an understanding of humankind as having a dual origin. It was psychotherapist Karlfried Graf Durckheim's view that humankind is child of both heaven and earth. We participate in both an earthly order and a heavenly order. The possibility of spiritual guidance, as a human activity in service to another, entails some discernment of where an individual's "center of gravity" lies between these two realms. Spiritual growth is another name for the formation of "magnetic center" oriented toward God. The term "magnetic center" appears in literature drawing on the teachings of the Russian saint, Theophan the Recluse (d. 1894). To understand how the two realms are related, recall these words of St. John the Baptist about the Christ: "He must increase, but I must decrease." (John 3:30) For some limited reference to the dual origins of humanity in Durckheim, see Ursula Wirtz, *Trauma and Beyond: The Mystery of Transformation* (London: Routledge, 2020). In Christianity there is an understanding of Jesus Christ as having two wills (in addition to two natures). The intuition of humankind as having dual origins is also a generalization of the dogma of Chalcedon.

[93] Isaiah 45:7 as rendered by Jean-Yves Leloup in his *Judas and Jesus: Two Faces of a Single Revelation*, translated into English by Joseph Rowe (Rochester, Vermont: Inner Traditions, 2007), p. 147.

[94] Salman Bashier, *Ibn al-'Arabi's Barzakh: The Concept of the Limit and the Relationship Between God and the World* (New York: State University of New York Press, 2004).

[95] In psychoanalytics there is both personal shadow and collective shadow.

consequence of human ecstasy. An unidentified writer has offered this description of the liminal condition:

> The word liminality has its origin in Latin and describes the ambiguity one feels in the middle of a transition from one state or status to another. An individual belongs neither to the condition one has left, nor to the one which comes next. [...] The whole world is now in a state of liminality. We are like the blind man at the pool (John 5:1-9), waiting for the Angel of Hope and Healing to disturb the waters. How long do we have to wait for a miracle? Yet, who knows how long the blind man had waited there, before the command came to pick up his bed and just walk? Each of us will have to choose how we live in this liminal space. And, despite being physically separated, we must embrace our shared humanity and the shared experience of facing the unknown together. We reach out to others who are struggling on the threshold betwixt and between a new normal. We dive deep into the stillness that has been forced upon us to discover the Eternal Presence that is always waiting there. We learn anew what it means to trust.
>
> The great Russian saint Maria Skobtsova [d. 1945] once described most beautifully what this trust is like: "It is possible to walk on dry land: to measure, to weigh, and to plan ahead. But it is also possible to walk on the waters. Then it becomes impossible to measure or to plan ahead. The one thing necessary is to believe all the time. An instant of doubt, and you begin to sink." If believing every moment is what it takes, then let us learn how to walk on water.[96]

This sensation of walking on the waters is precisely, also, the reality of our true condition. The liminal is also a kind of virtuality that has a becomingness but no actual being. To persist in this state is something like a failure to be born—a failure to become fully human.[97] This is a

---

[96] From an unsourced and undated paper, "On Liminality," in this author's possession.

[97] See my book, *The Anthropocosmic Vision: For a New Dialogic Civilization*, a Perennials Study Group publication, Memphis, Tennessee (CreateSpace, 2017), for an account of the virtuality that leads to a "human exit." My book, *The Anthropocosmic Vision*, based on the philosophical insights of the Russian

failure of realization. The liminal condition is most accurately characterized as the "place" of transformation.[98] We might usefully recall the saying of St. Gregory of Nyssa that "We are in some manner our own parents, giving birth to ourselves by our own free choice in accordance with whatever we wish to be, whether male or female, molding ourselves to the teaching of virtue or vice."[99]

There is a stillness in the liminal state—walking on water, for example, requires a certain stillness. For a different kind of example, consider this from the *Gospel of Mary Magdalene*, where Mary recounts her vision of Jesus—after His death and prior to His resurrection. In her vision, Jesus said to her: "You are blessed, Mary, since the sight of me *does not disturb you*. For where the heart is, there is the treasure."[100] Both Jesus and Mary were, at that moment, in a liminal state. This is a particular kind of stillness—a stillness that is an alert awareness, free of any precipitated or reactive trains of thought. It is objective witnessing as opposed to judging. In the terminology of John Vervaeke, it is a kind of "presencing" as opposed to "representing" (or "re-presenting").[101]

The experience of bewilderment is a sign of having entered a liminal state or condition. Professor of English, Ian Almond (George-

---

philosopher, Sergey Horujy, considers the significance of the malleability or porosity of the human border. This connects with the Mobius strip-like terminology used in this present book.

[98] We have referred several times above to "place" (sometimes, but not always, in quotes) that is also no-place, that is, without spatial coordinates. Henry Corbin discusses this phenomenon ("the country of non-where") in his 1972 paper, "*Mundus Imaginalis* or the Imaginary and the Imaginal," where he writes: "Henceforth, spiritual reality envelops, surrounds, contains so-called material reality. Spiritual reality can therefore not be found 'in the where.' The 'where' is in it. In other words, spiritual reality itself is the 'where' of all things." This paper can be found on-line at: <http://www.bahaistudies.net/asma/mundus_imaginalis.pdf> (Accessed 6/22/2020)

[99] Abraham J. Malherbe and Everett Ferguson, editors, Gregory of Nyssa, *The Life of Moses*, The Classics of Western Spirituality (Mahwah, New Jersey: Paulist Press, 1978), pp. 55-56.

[100] Lynn C. Bauman, Ward J. Bauman, Cynthia Bourgeault, *The Luminous Gospels: Thomas, Mary Magdalene, and Philip* (Telephone, Texas: Praxis Publishing, 2008), p. 67. Emphasis added.

[101] John Vervaeke in video conversation with Iain McGilchrist, previously cited.

town University, Qatar), writes: "Bewilderment takes place when we realize that our rational faculties are not enough to understand what is happening. That something has taken place in a language our rational faculties do not speak. In a sense, bewilderment takes place *because* of our rationality, because we insist on clinging to something that is blinding us to the 'actual situation.'"[102] The story, in Benedictine tradition, of Saints Maurus and Placid (6th century), contains another illustration of this liminal condition of walking on water:

> On a certain day, as venerable Benedict was in his cell, young Placidus, the holy man's monk, went out to take up water at the lake, and, putting down his pail carelessly, fell in after it. The water forthwith carried him away from the land as far as one may shoot an arrow. The man of God, being in his cell, by and by knew this. He called in haste for Maurus, saying: "Brother Maurus, run as fast as you can, for Placidus, who went to the lake to fetch water, has fallen in, and is carried a good way off."
>
> A strange thing, and, since the time of Peter the Apostle, never heard of! Maurus asked his father's blessing and, departing in all haste at his command, ran to that spot on the water to which the young lad had been carried by the force of the water. Thinking that he had all that while been on the land, Maurus took fast hold of Placidus by the hair of his head, in all haste he returned with him. As soon as he was on land, coming to himself, he looked back, and then knew very well that he had run on the water. That which before he dared not to presume, being now done and past, he both marveled at, and was afraid of what he had done.
>
> Coming back to the father, Benedict, and telling him what had happened, the venerable man did not attribute this to his own merits, but to the obedience of Maurus. Maurus, on the contrary, said that it was done only on his commandment, and that he had nothing to do with that miracle, not knowing at that time what he did. The friendly contention proceeded in mutual humility, but the youth himself that had been saved from drow-

[102] Ian Almond, "The Honesty of the Perplexed: Derrida and Ibn 'Arabi on Bewilderment," *Journal of the American Academy of Religion*, Volume 70, Issue 3, September 2002, pp. 515–537, pp. 515-516. Abstract on-line at: <https://doi.org/10.1093/jaar/70.3.515> (Accessed 8/11/2020)

ning determined the fact. He said that when he was drawn out of the water, he saw the Abbot's garment on his head, affirming thereby that it was the man of God that had delivered him from that great danger.[103]

As this story illustrates, when miracles happen, it is never of one's own doing.

<u>The way down is the way up.</u> The essential reality of reverie, it seems to me, is descent from the head and its mental activity into the heart as threshold—between time and eternity and at the intersections of other similar pairs.[104] To approach this threshold that is the heart is to enter the liminal condition. Consider these lines from T. S. Eliot:

> At the still point of the turning world. Neither flesh nor
>   fleshless;
> Neither from nor towards; at the still point, there the dance is,
> But neither arrest nor movement. And do not call it fixity,
> Where past and future are gathered. Neither movement from
>   nor towards,
> Neither ascent nor decline. Except for the point, the still point,
> There would be no dance, and there is only the dance.
> I can only say, *there* we have been: but I cannot say where.
> And I cannot say, how long, for that is to place it in time.[105]

Note the reference in these lines to the still point and to the dance. As we descend into the vicinity of the heart, we come closer to that still

---

[103] From *The Dialogues* of Saint Gregory the Great, Pope of Rome, Book Two: Life of Benedict, Chapter Seven. On-line at: <http://archive.osb.org/gen/greg/dia-09.html> (Accessed 1/16/2021)

[104] For the science of the heart's interconnectedness, see the work of the HeartMath Institute. On-line at: <https://www.heartmath.org/> (Accessed 7/6/2020). See also Heart Rhythm Meditation as taught by Puran Bair of iamHeart, Institute for Applied Meditation on the Heart. On-line at: <https://www.iamheart.org/> (Accessed 7/12/2020)

[105] From T. S. Eliot, "Burnt Norton" (No. 1 of "Four Quartets"). On-line at: <http://www.davidgorman.com/4quartets/1-norton.htm> (Accessed 6/29/2020)

point.[106] The *contents* of awareness (images and thoughts) are what we may call the dance. Our connection, however, through the still point, is to the *context* of awareness. In reversed perspective, d*escent* into the heart is also what is called *ascension*. Ascension is not aimless dream which has something unconscious about it. Ascension is fully conscious and *visionary*. Using evocative verbal imagery, the Christian poet and sage, Robert Lax, writes:

> The cosmos was born in joyful love
> and toward joyful love we are heading…
> It's "one spaceship" as they say.
> I think that we are moving toward
> a more unified, loving universe
> as we journey to the stars.[107]

What is sometimes called "waking dream" is an ambiguous state or condition for this reason.[108] In literature from widely varying spiritual cultures, we find instances of "visionary recitals." One such instance is the visionary recital of Mary Magdalene that appears in Dialogue Three of the *Gospel of Mary Magdalene*. Here are the concluding words of Mary's recital as it is presented in this Gospel:

> And my soul sang: "What bound me has been slain. What encompassed me has been vanquished. Desire has reached its end and I am freed from Ignorance. I left one world behind with the aid of another, and now as Image I have been freed from the analog. I am liberated from the chains of forgetfulness which have existed in time. From this moment onward,

---

[106] For a good description of the nature of the peacefulness in the vicinity of the still point, see Vincent Rossi, "Uncreated Peace: The 'Peace that passeth all understanding' according to the *Philokalia*," *Sophia: The Journal of Traditional Studies*, Volume 9, Number 1, Summer 2003. On-line at: <https://www.academia.edu/11378867/Uncreated_Peace_the_Peace_that_passeth_all_understanding_according_to_the_Philokalia> (Accessed 7/4/2020)

[107] As quoted in S. T. Georgiou, *Mystic Street: Meditations on a Spiritual Path* (Ottawa, Canada: Novalis, 2007), p. 305.

[108] For the place of waking dream within the context of therapeutics, see the work of the Kabbalist, Colette Aboulker-Muskat (d. 2003), as taught in the United States by the late Dr. Gerald Epstein and others.

I go forward into the season of the Great Age, the Aeon, and there, where time rests in stillness in the Eternity of time, I will repose in silence." And having said this Mary fell silent since it was to this point that the Savior had brought her.[109]

This is also Mary's song of freedom. Although she has overcome those forces that resist her (visionary) ascent into freedom, the emphasis is on liberty rather than liberation. The journey is an inner one. A significant resource for ascension is the simple rosary—an effective key for unlocking the gates of many prisons because the rosary and its reveries are beyond the control of any authorities.[110] Readers of this book may remember this key when attending to the final section of this book, Section 10 ("Leaving Babylon"), concerned with the oppressive and death-dealing mechanisms of our present civilization. This even includes culture insofar as culture serves the *status quo*—keeping things as they are—and contributes to the "sleep" of populations.[111]

The threshold of the heart is also the place of exchange—an exchange of the created and the uncreated energies within (the created and the uncreated) Sophia of God. There is here, in the language of Cynthia Bourgeault, "an openness to giving and receiving in a framework that embraces everything—information, goods, energy, sus-

---

[109] *The Luminous Gospels*, pp. 68-69. Note the words "silence" and "silent" in this excerpt. If the heart functions as a kind of "homing device," the signal that it listens for may seem to be the profoundest silence.

[110] Of all the many available books concerned with the rosary, Robert Llewelyn's *A Doorway to Silence: Contemplative Use of the Rosary* (London: Darton, Longman and Todd, 1986) is especially commended. Llewelyn's brief notes on "Introducing a Rosary of Peace" can be found on-line here: <http://www.annunciationtrust.org.uk/prayercards/Introducing%20A%20Rosary%20of%20of%20Peace.pdf> (Accessed 11/16/2020). For uses of the rosary beyond Christian contexts, see Clark Strand and Perdita Finn, *The Way of the Rose: The Radical Path of the Divine Feminine Hidden in the Rosary* (New York: Spiegel & Grau, 2019).

[111] In the condition of "sleep," people are moved along the path of least resistance—in a "downward" direction along the Ray of Creation—toward their final destination and end as "food for the moon," in Gurdjieff's terminology. This is the negative sense of "downward," not to be confused with the positive sense also discussed in this book section.

tenance, etc."[112] This framework is a metaphysics of Christian wisdom. In this wisdom, there is gradual re-centering "down," from the head into the heart. As an aspect of this metaphysics, attention is called to "the noetic faculty, the faculty that enables direct apprehension of the presence of God,"[113] in the language of Peter Brooke, Orthodox Christian, painter and writer on various topics. We will see the relevance of this as we come to our discussion of Saint Symeon the New Theologian at Section 9 further below.[114]

One of the images in the collage of images on the cover of this book is the *Salvatore Mundi* by Leonardo da Vinci. In this painting the Christ holds in his left hand a glass or crystal orb.[115] Integral spiritual psychologist and author, Robert Sardello (The School of Spiritual Psychology), has had some insightful things to say about this painting and about the symbolism of the orb. He says "the way is now down":

The painting—the very extraordinary painting by Leonardo, shows the way of self-awakening in combination with Spiritual-Earth awakening. *Salvator Mundi*, the Savior of the World, was painted in 1500; it disappeared in the 17th century until it was found and restored from 2005-2008 and exhibited for the first time on November 11, 2011. It sold for $450 million dollars, purchased by Abdullah bin Farhan Al Saud, to be placed in the Louvre Abu Dhabi. Thus far, it has not been displayed. …

There is now a way down to the Divine Soul, imagined as at the center of the earth rather than in the heavens. The true secret of this painting, at least from the imagining of an integral spiritual psychology (no art critic or expert has seen the painting in this way), is found with the clear crystal orb Christ holds

---

[112] From the description of "The Divine Exchange," a 14-week course offered in 2020 by the *Center for Action and Contemplation*. Course description on-line at: <https://cac.org/the-divine-exchange/> (Accessed 6/30/2020)

[113] This language is found in Peter Brooke, "Nicholas Laos on Orthodoxy," an essay at Peter Brooke's website. On-line at: <http://www.peterbrooke.org/politics-and-theology/orthodoxy-index/laos.html> (Accessed 7/4/2020)

[114] Among monks on Mount Athos associated with the Kollyvades movement, there was enthusiastic response, from the 18th century until today, to the teachings of the late Medieval Byzantine saint, Symeon the New Theologian (d. 1022). See Hannah Hunt, *A Guide to St. Symeon the New Theologian* (Eugene, Oregon: Wipf and Stock / Cascade Books, 2015), p. 106.

[115] As may be obvious, paintings may serve as springboards for reverie.

in his left hand. The orb is a mysterious alteration of the more usual form of an orb surmounted by a cross. The orb is understood as the Earth. But, this orb is transparent. Get that one—this orb is transparent, that is to say invisible—the invisible Earth, the Spiritual-Earth.

Look at … a crystal orb…. In an orb, the heavens and the Earth are reversed; the heavens are down and Earth is up. The way down is the way up! And the way up is the way down! That is, *Salvator Mundi* is saying, the way is now down—to the Divine Soul. Because of depth psychology, we do not consider 'down' as the way to the Divine Soul, but rather to the so-called unconscious. The error of depth psychology has obscured coming into the presence of the Divine Soul. How to begin the journey? The way of receptivity, the Feminine way.[116]

The reader may also call to mind the Tarot card known as "The Hanged Man" that may serve as further occasion for reflecting on the notion of reversed perspective. The anonymous writer of *Meditations on the Tarot* writes this in his Letter XII:

Who is the Hanged Man? Is he a saint, a righteous man, an initiate? He can certainly be regarded as all three, for all three have in common that their will is an organ of heaven, but what he is most especially, what he represents individually, is neither sanctity, nor righteousness, nor initiation, but something which is their synthesis. The Hanged Man is the *eternal Job*, tried and tested from century to century, who represents humanity towards God and God towards humanity. The Hanged Man is the *truly human man* and his lot is a truly human one. The Hanged Man is the representative of humanity who is found between two kingdoms—that of this world and that of heaven. For that which is truly human in man and in humanity is the Hanged Man.[117]

---

116 Robert Sardello, "The Truth of the Way Down," May 23, 2020, a blog entry at his website. On-line at: <http://www.robertsardello.com/blog/may-23rd-2020> (Accessed 7/1/2020)
117 Anonymous, *Meditations on the Tarot: A Journey into Christian Hermeticism*, translated by Robert Powell (New York: Jeremy P. Tarcher / Putnam, 2002),

The way down is also a way in. As we are considering the properties of the glass or crystal orb, here is one further illumination and that is that we humankind are *in* (*inside*) the orb that is Earth. By "Earth" we mean not simply the ground under our feet, but the Earth as inclusive of the air and the clouds above us—the entirety of the living Gaia. The Earth orb in which we live extends some miles above our heads.[118]

We find ourselves in the liminal state of being between two waters—the waters above and the waters below—with (interior and exterior) rain as connection between these two waters. We have elsewhere named the rains of grace and inner tears as *dralas* that are phenomena that transcend any neat distinction between "inner" and "outer."[119] Consider the places where water figures in the Biblical narrative. In the Old Testament, there is the story of Noah and the flood waters. There is also the story of Yahweh parting the waters of the Red Sea for Moses and the Hebrew people. There is a speaking to the rock versus a striking of the rock. In connection with Jesus healing someone, there is mud placed on the eyes. There is the pool of Siloam. These are all energetic images—energies ascending and descending.

Lee van Laer, a senior editor at *Parabola* magazine, writes about the two directions from which the human tree sustains its life—the above and the below:

> Hadewijch's roots of Charity, the foundational source of love, are *drawn down into God*.
>
> What does this mean?
>
> Gurdjieff told Ouspensky that a human being must develop in both directions in order to become whole; no connection to the level above a human being can develop without a corresponding and equally powerful development to the level below him. In saying this, he touched on the many ancient mythologies which view the metaphysics of the soul as a tree whose

---

p. 337. It is generally recognized that the actual author of this work is the Estonian-Russian Christian hermeticist, Valentin Tomberg (d. 1973).

[118] According to the Center for Science Education, Earth's atmosphere has a series of layers that are named the troposphere (lowest layer), stratosphere, mesosphere, thermosphere and exosphere (highest layer).

[119] Some reference to *dralas* appears in each of my first three books: *From Glory to Glory: The Sophianic Vision of Fr. Sergius Bulgakov* (2016), *The Anthropocosmic Vision: For a New Dialogic Civilization* (2017), and *Taliesin's Harp* (2019).

branches reach into heaven and whose roots reach deep in the earth; yet those roots reach for God the below human being in exactly the same way that they reach for God above him, because God creates all levels and exists in equal measure within each one of them.

A human being cannot be charitable unless the *roots* of their being, the *sensory contacts which feed themselves on the basis of a man's or woman's existence*, are developed in love. That love must be fundamental as an inner source of nourishment, not a love of the world and its things, but a love that begins before the world exists.[120]

The notion of our life between two realms—the waters above and the waters below—are encapsulated in van Laer's words. The divine is not simply "upward"—it is also "downward," as we have suggested in this section. This bi-directionality values the senses. The unitive vision does not entail a view of the manifest world as fundamentally or entirely illusory. It is rather the "play" of the divine enjoyment in veiling and unveiling the divine light or glory and the divine mystery. The Old Testament image of Jacob's ladder upon which angels are ascending and descending is an apt image of the continuous energetic exchange that transpires between the worlds. The human being is the channel of these energies.[121] As we shall see in the next section, below, the tree, with its branches above and its roots below, is a glyph or revelatory image of ourselves as that "place" wherein the worlds embrace. This, too, is reverie—wherein the worlds embrace.

According to Herman Green (Center for Ecozoic Studies), it was the view of Thomas Berry (d. 2009), cultural historian and scholar of world religions, that it has been the task of Western cultures to perform three mediations:

---

[120] From "Drawn Down Into God," essay by Lee van Laer at his blog, *Zen, Yoga, Gurdjieff—Perspectives on Inner Work.*, September 21, 2019. On-line at: <http://zenyogagurdjieff.blogspot.com/2019/09/drawn-down-into-god.html> (Accessed 11/9/2020). The emphases appear in the original.

[121] It was Gurdjieff's insight that humans contribute to world maintenance when they are fully awake (not in states of "sleep") and their energies are therefore counter-entropic. The twin pillars of our spiritual obligation in this regard are conscious labor and intentional suffering.

The first was that between the divine and the human. It began in ancient Israel, continued in the early Christian community, and then was communicated to Mohammed. The second mediation began following the industrial revolution when people were divided into different classes, nation-states became dominant, contact between peoples increased, and conflicts ensued. The second mediation concerned inter-human affairs. The third mediation became necessary in the 20th century and continues through today. This mediation is between the human community and Earth. It is important in itself and, in Berry's view, now the inter-human mediation and the divine-human mediation are also dependent on it.[122]

Mediation as conscious task is more effective when the mediation is imaginatively discerned as a possibility. This is a function of reverie.

5. Trees and the Green Man

Giant oak with man

And in paradise five evergreen trees await you. They do not change in summer nor shed their leaves in winter. If you come to know them, you will not know the taste of death.[123]
— Logion 19b, *The Gospel of Thomas*

---

[122] Herman Greene, "The Long View: Thomas Berry's Instruction on the Reform of Religion, Law, and Culture in His Later Books," Center for Ecozoic Studies, website post, undated. On-line at: <https://www. ecozoicstudies.org/reviews/the-long-view-thomas-berrys-instruction-on-the-reform-of-religion-law-and-culture-in-his-later-books/> (Accessed 1/23/2021)

[123] *The Luminous Gospels*, p. 15. There is no consensus on the meaning of the "five trees." Some have suggested possible Kabbalistic parallels with five soul levels or with five worlds (counting Adam Kadmon as the first or the fifth).

We said above that *symbology* is one of the ways that Heaven communicates with Earth. We used the term *symbology* in preference to the simpler term symbol because what we are pointing, not to something static, but to something with which we are invited to exercise *discernment*. The tree is a primordial image—a regulative image—that rewards attention. It is an object of reverie, as the human person is an object of reverie, in the sense that these both invite and reward our contemplation. In another sense, the tree is *not* the true object of reverie. It is simply a doorway, albeit a primordial one, to some more comprehensive "object" ontologically nearer to the attractive and magnetic human *telos*.

Rublev's icon of the Trinity is one of the most perfect images I can think of that can serve as image of the reveriesial state or condition or process.[124] This icon is based on the Old Testament story or vignette of the three angels who visit Abraham (Genesis 18:1-8). The visit occurs near the Oak of Mamre. So we have a tree in the story but, rather than being a focus of the visit or of the story, the visit or meeting occurs in the vicinity of the oak. In the icon, the angels are in a deeply contemplative state. They are not speaking; words have dropped away. The tree appears in the icon, but it does not call attention to itself. Among the angelic visitors, there is mutual deference. This is also how reverie proceeds—one presentation or intimation giving way to another. What enables this? What holds all this together as one coherent occasion? It is—in this place, in this moment—the descent of the Kingdom. It is also the manifestation of the House of Love.[125] The Dutch Catholic priest, professor, author and theologian, Henri Nouwen (d. 1996), wrote about this icon as follows:

---

[124] Another image might be Botticelli's painting, *Primavera* ("Spring") in the Uffizi Gallery, Florence. This painting is thought to have been created in the late 1470s or early 1480s.

[125] Anthony de Mello S.J. said: "Some say that there are only two things in the world: God and fear; love and fear are the only two things. There's only one evil in the world, fear. There's only one good in the world, love. It's sometimes called by other names. It's sometimes called happiness or freedom or peace or joy or God or whatever. But the label doesn't really matter. And there's not a single evil in the world that you cannot trace to fear. Not one." From *Awareness: A de Mello Spirituality Conference in His Own Words* (New York: Doubleday, 1992). On-line at: <http://www.arvindguptatoys.com/ arvindgupta/tonyawareness.pdf> (Accessed 10/31/2020)

Saint Sergius, in whose honor and memory Rublev painted the Trinity icon, wanted to bring all of Russia together around the Name of God so that its people would conquer "the devouring hatred of the world by the contemplation of the Holy Trinity."

Fear and hatred have become no less destructive since the 14th century, and Rublev's icon has become no less creative in calling us to the place of love, where fear and hatred no longer can destroy us. The longer we pray with the icon and the deeper our heart is drawn toward that mysterious place where circle and cross are both present, the more fully we come to understand how to be committed to the struggle for justice and peace in the world while remaining at home in God's love….

I pray that Rublev's icon will teach many how to live in the midst of a fearful, hateful and violent world while moving always deeper into the house of love.[126]

Trees are a central element of the cosmic revelation. As with revelation in general, all aspects of the revelation are significant. In this instance—the instance of trees—all elements of trees are significant, whether we are considering their roots and branches or their leaves and fruit. The roots of trees and other plants bring to mind the observations of Simone Weil on the similar need of humankind for roots:

To be rooted is perhaps the most important and least recognized need of the human soul. It is one of the hardest to define. A human being has roots by virtue of his real, active and natural participation in the life of a community which preserves in living shape certain particular treasures of the past and certain particular expectations for the future. This participation is a natural one, in the sense that it is automatically brought about by place, conditions of birth, profession and social surroundings. Every human being needs to have multiple roots. It is necessary for one to draw well-nigh the whole of one's moral, intellectual and spiritual life by way of the environment of which one forms a natural part.

Reciprocal exchanges by which different sorts of environment exert influence on one another are no less vital than to be

---

126 Henri J. M. Nouwen, *Behold the Beauty of the Lord: Praying with Icons* (Notre Dame, Indiana: Ave Maria Press, 1987), pp. 26-27.

rooted in natural surroundings. But a given environment should not receive an outside influence as something additional to itself, but as a stimulant intensifying its own particular way of life. It should draw nourishment from outside contributions only after having digested these, and the human beings who compose it should receive such contributions only from its hands. When a really talented painter walks into a picture gallery, their own originality is thereby confirmed. The same thing should apply to the various communities throughout the world and the different social environments.[127]

The prophet Jeremiah had, long ago, said this: "Blessed are those who trust in the Lord, whose trust is the Lord. They shall be like a tree planted by water, sending out its roots by the stream. It shall not fear when heat comes, and its leaves shall stay green; in the year of drought it is not anxious, and it does not cease to bear fruit."[128]

Both as individuals and as community, it is clear that our life is not sustainable without "root work"—taking care of our roots. It is reverie that enables access to the cosmic revelation. Consider these lines from the German lyric poet and writer, Hilde Domin (d. 2006):

> We must be able to go away
> and yet be like a tree
> rooted in the earth
> standing fast while the landscape passes.
> We must hold our breath
> until the wind dies down
> and different air starts to encircle us
> until the play of light and shade
> of green and blue
> shows the old pattern

---

[127] Simone Weil, *The Need for Roots: Prelude to a Declaration of Duties towards Mankind,* translated by Arthur Wills (London: Routledge, 2002), p. 40. On-line at: <https://antilogicalism.com/wp-content/uploads/2019/04/need-roots.pdf> (Accessed 9/13/2020). Lightly edited here, for inclusive language. For human rootedness in the natural and constructed worlds, see the work of Christopher Alexander, referenced further below in this present text at footnote 236, page 114, further below.

[128] Jeremiah 17:7-8 (NRSV).

and we are home
wherever that may be
and able to sit down and lean against it
as if it were the gravestone of
our mother.[129]

One may recall these brief lines of dialogue in Antoine de Saint Exupéry's novella, *The Little Prince*:

The little prince crossed the desert and met with only one
flower. It was a flower with three petals, a flower of no
account at all.
"Good morning," said the little prince.
"Good morning," said the flower.
"Where are the men?" the little prince asked, politely.
The flower had once seen a caravan passing.
"Men?" she echoed. "I think there are six or seven of them in
existence. I saw them, several years ago. But one never knows
where to find them. The wind blows them away. They have
no roots, and that makes their life very difficult."
"Goodbye," said the little prince.
"Goodbye," said the flower.[130]

We appear to lack roots. If this is true, it is bad for us, indeed—because without roots, there is no life. Where are our roots? We have the capacity to develop roots, but not the guarantee.[131]

Both trees and gardens are associated with paradise in whatever religious tradition we may be concerned with.[132] Reverie is a name of

---

[129] This poem is titled "Passing Landscape" in English translation by Meg Taylor and Elke Heckel. On-line at: <http://hildedomin.megtaylor.co.uk/translations-1#PassingLandscape> (Accessed 9/13/2020)

[130] Chapter 18 in Antoine de Saint-Exupéry's *The Little Prince* (New York: Reynal & Hitchcock, 1943) as translated from the French by Katherine Woods. On-line at: <http://blogs.ubc.ca/edcp508/files/2016/02/TheLittlePrince.pdf> (Accessed 11/23/2020)

[131] Elsewhere in this present text the dual origins of humankind are noted. Using the terminology of Gurdjieff, we might say that as we live in Earth (World 48) we have the capacity to send roots into the Heavenly realm (World 24). If, however, we fail to do this, we may become "food for the moon."

that reciprocal opening that is intended by the word *love*.[133] As Thomas Merton understood, true poets are gifted with the "paradise ear." He writes:

> All really valid poetry (poetry that is fully alive, and asserts its reality by its power to generate imaginative life) is a kind of recovery of paradise. Not that the poet comes up with a report that he, an unusual man, has found his own way back into Eden; but the living line and the generative association, the new sound, the music, the structure, are somehow grounded in a renewal of vision and hearing so that he who reads and understands recognizes that here is a new start, a new creation.[134]

It is worth underscoring what may seem so obvious as not worth mentioning and that is the capacity of forests of trees to heal maladies of heart and soul.[135] The same can be said about gardens. Consider the gardens—the Eden from which we have come and the New Eden toward which we are journeying. Our movement out of the first garden and our movement toward the second garden are each a consequence of our connection to a tree. In Adam, we were expelled from the first garden because we ate fruit of the Tree of Knowledge (of the dualities, including good and evil) but the garden re-appears as we

---

[132] For a survey of Christian understanding of paradise in history, literature, and art, see Rita Nakashima Brock and Rebecca Ann Parker, *Saving Paradise: How Christianity Traded Love of This World for Crucifixion and Empire* (Boston: Beacon Press, 2008).

[133] As pointed out by John Vervaeke in conversation with Iain McGilchrist, previously cited. The observation was made as a contrast to reciprocal closing (or narrowing) of the scope of awareness in addictions.

[134] As quoted in George Kilcourse, "'The Paradise Ear': Thomas Merton, Poet," *The Kentucky Review*, Summer 1987, Volume 7, Number 2, Article 8, pp. 98-121, p. 119.

[135] For information about the practice of forest therapy, visit the website of the Association of Nature and Forest Therapy Guides and Programs at: <https://www.natureandforesttherapy.org/> (Accessed 7/5/2020). An *International Handbook of Forest Therapy* (2019) is available from Cambridge Scholars Publishing: <https://www.cambridgescholars.com/international-handbook-of-forest-therapy> (Accessed 7/5/2020).

eat fruit of the Tree of Life (which is unitive understanding).[136] As Samuel Zinner points out, "… the Tree of Life is associated with the Virgin Mary in Christian symbolism."[137]

In a deeper and more important sense, Jesus Christ is also associated with the Tree of Life, understood as *Axis Mundi* (axis of the world).[138] He is, in a deep sense, the mediation of Heaven and Earth. He is the measure by which all else is measured. He is the touchstone of reality. As such, Christ is *the* object of reverie—that before which we allow dream to manifest and coalesce. In this dream, which may become waking dream, we live. We inhabit the dream.

All these trees grace our dreams. The silver and gold trees with their leaves and fruit are an emblem of our paradise.[139] The willow trees associate with the weeping and other sorrows of death. The fig trees are forever associated with Our Lord's teaching and warning. The sycamore tree elevated Zacchaeus so that he could see the Lord. Lombardy poplars, tall and stately, bring to mind my grandparents' home and yard in rural Mississippi. The hanging tree and the Cross of crucifixion—these, too, mark our human suffering and the suffering of the trees. Even the trees have their reverie. The Dream of the Rood is a reverie of the tree in the bitter sweetness of its suffering. Roots of a felled tree may revive. In Jamaica today there is a tree, locally referred to as the "TreeALife," under which a Rastafarian sage chooses to

---

[136] See the lovely story as told by Thomas Atum O'Kane in a short video titled, "In the Garden of Well-Being." On-line at: <https://youtu.be/ zc01hmOMb0Q> (Accessed 7/14/2020). In Atum O'Kane's telling, there are inner gardens as well as outer gardens.

[137] Samuel Zinner, *Christianity and Islam: Essays on Ontology and Archetype* (London, U.K.: The Matheson Trust for the Study of Comparative Religion, 2010), p. 225.

[138] See Mario Baghos, "Christ, Paradise, Trees, and the Cross in the Byzantine Art of Italy," *International Journal of Orthodox Theology*, 2018, Volume 9, Issue 2, pp. 112-155. On-line at: <https://www.academia.edu/37603531/Christ_ Paradise_Trees_and_the_Cross_in_the_Byzantine_Art_of_Italy> (Accessed 9/30/2020). In Norse cosmology, *Yggdrasil* is the name of the world tree that connects the nine worlds.

[139] In the legendarium of J. R. R. Tolkien, Telperion and Laurelin are the Two Trees of Valinor, the Silver Tree and the Gold Tree, which brought light to Valinor. Angelic beings lived in this paradisal realm also known as the Undying Lands.

convene his occasional "reasonings." In the Qur'an there is a chapter (*sura*) that contains what is known as the Verse of Light:

> Allah is the Light of the heavens and the earth. The parable of His Light is a niche wherein is a lamp—the lamp is in a glass, the glass as it were a glittering star—lit from a blessed olive tree, neither eastern nor western, whose oil almost lights up, though fire should not touch it. Light upon light. Allah guides to His Light whomever He wishes. Allah draws parables for mankind and Allah has knowledge of all things.[140]

Trees containing hollow space have sometimes served as hermitage or oratory for solitary prayer. Trees also provide shelter—to the birds, other animals, and to humans who seek out forests in which to grieve, to heal, or even to die. (See the reference further below to the church forests in Ethiopia.) The monks of the monastic community (skete) that grew up around the Russian saint, Nilus of Sora (d. 1508), lived in a forest environment. Trees provide the wood for Noah's ark. The desert shrub that Moses saw—the Burning Bush, the fiery shrub that was not consumed—has also become an emblem of the Blessed Virgin Mary. Every object is a Burning Bush—for those who have eyes to see the interior fire in all things.

All trees are pointers to Paradise.[141] What can be said about Paradise? For Symeon the New Theologian, faith is "the New Paradise" and love is "the Holy Sion not made with hands."[142] Here are words from the Greek lay theologian, Alexander Kalomiros (d. 1990):

> Do not seek to understand God for it is impossible. Simply open the door of your soul so His presence may fill you and

---

[140] *Qu'ran*, Sura 24, Verse 35. Ali Quli Qara'i translation.

[141] For in-depth look at the significance of trees in Medieval Britain, see Michael D. J. Bintley, *Trees in the Religions of Early Medieval England* (Woodbridge, Suffolk, U.K.: The Boydell Press, 2015) and Della Hooke, *Trees in Anglo-Saxon England: Literature, Lore and Landscape* (Woodbridge, Suffolk, U.K.: The Boydell Press, 2010). Both of these titles are volumes in the publisher's Anglo-Saxon Studies series.

[142] As cited by Constantine Carvarnos in his *The Hellenic-Christian Philosophical Tradition* (Belmont, Massachusetts: Institute for Byzantine and Modern Greek Studies, 1989), p. 33.

illumine your mind and heart, warm your body, and enter your veins. Theology is not a cerebral knowledge but a living knowledge that is directly relevant to man and sustains and possesses the whole man. A cold, cerebral man cannot know and discourse on divine things, even if his head contains an entire patristic library. He who is not moved by a sunset, a tree, or a bird cannot be stirred even by the Creator of these things. In order to grasp God and be able to talk about Him to others you must be a poetic soul. It means that you must have a heart that is noble, sensitive, and pure. You must be as an ear that is turned to the whisperings of the Infinite, and as an eye that sees through the bottomless depths while all other eyes see only pitch blackness. It is impossible for timorous souls and stingy hearts to discourse on divine things.

The heart that grasps the mysteries is one that is naive enough to think all souls worthy of Paradise, even souls who may have drenched their heart's life with bitterness. It is a heart that feels and sings like a bird, without caring if there is no one there to hear it. It rejoices over everything that is beautiful, everything that is true, because truth and beauty are two aspects of the same thing and can never be separated. It has compassion for every living thing that is animate or has roots, and even for every seemingly lifeless stone.

It is a modest soul that is out of its waters in the limelight of men but blooms in solitude and quiet. It is a heart free to its very roots, impervious to every kind of pressure, far from every kind of stench, untouched by any kind of chains. It distinguishes truth from false hood with a certain mystic sense. Its every breath offers gratitude for all of God's works that surround it and for every joy and every affliction, for every possession, and for every privation as well. Crouching humbly on the Cornerstone which is Christ, it drinks unceasingly of the eternal water of Paradise and utters the Name of Him who was and is ever merciful. Such a soul is like a shady tree by the running waters of the Church, with deep roots and a high crown where kindred souls find comfort and refuge in its dense branches.

Such is the true theologian. If anyone wishes to be so named, let him be measured by this measure. Even he who simply wishes to be a disciple of such theologians must walk in their exact footsteps if he desires their words to be echoed in himself, and his eyes to see light.[143]

And what of the Green Man? The Green Man is the presentiment and "voice" of inter-being. The Green Man is usually only perceptible when we are in some sort of liminal state, a state of receptivity. Otherwise, we perceive nothing but the leaves and the wind. We do not perceive the wind as the breath of God. We do not perceive the swaying leaves penetrated by the glimmering sunlight as the Green Man. The voice of inter-being speaks in various modes. To encounter the Green Man (Leaf Man) is to be presented with an invitation—an invitation that seems analogous to the invitation presented to the birds in the Persian Sufi story, *Conference of the Birds*. It is an invitation to find the Simorgh—or, in other words, the invitation to a search that is also a transformative journey.

Within Jewish spiritual cultures there is the glyph of the Tree of Life (in Kabbalah). Within Kabbalistic circles, when a person is in a particularly reflective state one may be said to "climb" the Tree of Life. Climbing the Tree of Life is what the Kabbalist does. This is a particular mode of reverie. There is, however, an ambiguity about the extent to which reverie is an active or a passive mode of awareness. What is called Merkabah (or Chariot) mysticism seems to be passively experienced and visionary. We may understand shamanic "travel," in indigenous cultural context, as a kinesthetically active mode of reverie. It is an active mode of reverie that is also mythically specific.

The Green Man knows where the water is—where the fountains are. Saint Clement of Alexandria wrote about these fountains: "It has been therefore said by inspiration: 'Hear, my son, and receive my words; that thine may be the many ways of life. For I teach thee the ways of wisdom; that the fountains fail thee not,' which gush forth from the earth itself."[144] What is this wisdom? It is the unveiling of connections—of our connection with every living thing.

---

[143] From Alexander Kalomiros, *Nostalgia for Paradise* (Ridgewood, New Jersey: Zephyr Publishing, English edition, 2006), as excerpted by Fr. Stephen Freeman at the *Glory to God for All Things* blog, February 15, 2014. On-line at: <https://blogs.ancientfaith.com/glory2godforallthings/2014/02/15/ nostalgia-for-paradise/> (Accessed 8/7/2020)

[144] Clement of Alexandria, *The Stromata, or Miscellanies*, Book 1, Chapter 5, in Alexander Roberts and James Donaldson, editors, *Ante-Nicene Fathers*, Volume

These connections are witness to humankind's obligation of sensitivity and care for all that lives. William Blake in his poem, "Auguries of Innocence," lays bare many of these inter-connections. While the entire poem is commended to the reader, here are the first lines:

To see a World in a Grain of Sand
And a Heaven in a Wild Flower
Hold Infinity in the palm of your hand
And Eternity in an hour
A Robin Red breast in a Cage
Puts all Heaven in a Rage
A Dove house filld with Doves & Pigeons
Shudders Hell thr' all its regions
A dog starvd at his Masters Gate
Predicts the ruin of the State
A Horse misusd upon the Road
Calls to Heaven for Human blood
Each outcry of the hunted Hare
A fibre from the Brain does tear
A Skylark wounded in the wing
A Cherubim does cease to sing
The Game Cock clipd & armd for fight
Does the Rising Sun affright
Every Wolfs & Lions howl
Raises from Hell a Human Soul
The wild deer, wandring here & there
Keeps the Human Soul from Care
The Lamb misusd breeds Public Strife
And yet forgives the Butchers knife
The Bat that flits at close of Eve
Has left the Brain that wont Believe
The Owl that calls upon the Night
Speaks the Unbelievers fright
He who shall hurt the little Wren

---

2 (Edinburgh: T&T Clark / Grand Rapids, MI: Wm. B. Eerdmans Publishing Company, reprinted 2001), p. 305. On-line at the Christian Classics Ethereal Library at: <https://ccel.org/ccel/schaff/anf02/anf02/Page_305.html> (Accessed 11/19/2020)

Shall never be belovd by Men
He who the Ox to wrath has movd
Shall never be by Woman lovd
The wanton Boy that kills the Fly
Shall feel the Spiders enmity
[…][145]

This is reverie as manifested in language. It is language that, if we let it, forms in us a certain keenness of vision and moral sensitivity. Using images certain to inspire reverie, Clement of Alexandria wrote as follows about the divine reality:

> Therefore also the Egyptians place Sphinxes before their temples, to signify that the doctrine respecting God is enigmatical and obscure; perhaps also that we ought both to love and fear the Divine Being: to love Him as gentle and benign to the pious; to fear Him as inexorably just to the impious; for the sphinx shows the image of a wild beast and of a man together.[146]

We humans are trees! Our roots are in Earth and our branches and leaves strain toward heaven, the celestial![147] We ourselves are the Green Man—as ephemeral as its breath of wind. Reveries are the unfolding of our myriad leaves in the light of the spiritual sun!

In our embodied life there is some "distance" between ourselves as we experience our life in the world and our origin, the place from which we have come and to which we return. This is why humankind, at some point in the distant past, acquired the capacity for stories. In the following section, we reflect on one such story.

---

[145] From William Blake, "Auguries of Innocence." The full text of the poem, as published in *Poets of the English Language* (Viking Press, 1950), can be found on-line at the Poetry Foundation website : <https://www.poetryfoundation. org/poems/43650/auguries-of-innocence> (Accessed 11/28/2020)

[146] From Clement of Alexandria, *The Stromata*, Book 5, Chapter 5, in *The Catholic Encyclopedia*. On-line at: <https://www.newadvent.org/fathers/ 02105.htm> (Accessed 12/2/2020)

[147] This connects with what is said elsewhere in this present text about humankind as having dual origins.

6. Discerning the Atlantean Heritage

Sphinxes and holy fire

Reverie is the primary and first expression of the primordial. Its character is wondrous and melodic. Atlantis can be understood as the implied common origin of all planetary wisdoms. Here is one statement of this deeply ecological point of view:

> Scythianos inspired a culture of music and song that spread over Europe, most probably from the north, so that we may connect it with Hyperborea. This is the common source of the Celtic bards, the Germanic scalds, and the Greek and Thracian singers that are associated with Apollo and Orpheus. The Finnish laulajat and the Russian skaziteli can be added to them. The harmonious music of this song culture created peace in the soul and it helped build the organs of thought.
>
> Hyperborea or Thule appears as the name for the islands between Newfoundland (Canada) and Scandinavia, among them Greenland, Iceland, and Ireland, as well as islands that sunk into the sea at the end of Atlantis. This was the northern part of Atlantis, that was not covered by ice. When the ice had melted, new lands appeared—Scandinavia, Finland and Northern Russia. Already during the Ice Age there may have been initiation centers here: on Spitsbergen (Svalbard), in Lapland, around the White Sea (possibly on the islands of Solovietsky in Russia), and on Nova Zembla. We may therefore include these new lands in the mystery land of Hyperborea.
>
> In Egypt and the Middle East, initiation led to knowledge of the inner world of man and the earth; in the North of Europe to knowledge of the outer world (nature and the cosmos).
>
> The sun oracle of Manu on Atlantis was not far from Ireland. Here, in the last phase of Atlantis, Manu prepared selected people for the development of thinking in the post-Atlantean age. From this oracle a network of initiation schools was

created in Europe. The initiation center that remained closest to the traditions of Atlantis was in Ireland.[148]

If the above account seems highly speculative, it is because this is how reverie "works." Reverie is the cauldron of Ceridwen that issues in all the modalities of language, from the mythical/historical to the poetic/visionary and metaphysical. It is this primordial reverie (that is both active and passive) that is intended or deeply implied in contemporary psycho-therapeutic and other uses of the term "imaginal." It forms us as a people in certain ways. It is recognized that images or, more generally, impressions have healing (or deleterious) effects. Gurdjieff had spoken of the "food of impressions." The psychiatrist, Dr. Gerald Epstein (d. 2019), together with his co-editor, Barbara Fedoroff, wrote:

> Simply put, imagery is the mind speaking to us in pictures. Like English, it is a language; but a picture language rather than a word language. Imagery conveys the higher wisdom of our minds and longing of our hearts. It is also how the mind "speaks" or instructs the body, so it is a natural healing modality. The imaginal experience comprises what we see, sense, feel, live and know. You may see images in color, black or white or shades of tone. Concurrently you may feel emotions such as joy or sadness, love or anger, etc. Likewise, you may physically sense in your body tingling, a rush of energy, constriction or relaxation of muscles, etc. Occasionally, you may hear sounds as well. In sum, imagery is the natural and true language of our inner life.[149]

Reverie, broadly considered, has to do with the play of phenomena, whether these phenomena are visual impressions or otherwise. The play of phenomena is ambiguous with respect to any agency implied in

---

[148] From "Journeying to Hyperborea, An Exploration of the Spiritual History and Future of Northern Europe," talks by Harrie Salman, as quoted in Douglas Gabriel, "Scythianos – the Hidden Master" (e-book), p. 13. On-line at: <https://neoanthroposophy.files.wordpress.com/2020/03/scythianos-hidden-master_douglas-gabriel.pdf> (Accessed 10/24/2020)

[149] Gerald Epstein and Barbara L. Fedoroff, editors, *The Encyclopedia of Mental Imagery: Colette Aboulker-Muscat's 2,100 Visualizations for Personal Development, Healing, and Self-knowledge* (New York, New York: ACMI Press, 2012), p. 4.

the phenomena. The play of phenomena is sometimes named *maya* in the spiritual traditions considered below. As the contents of conscious awareness, collectively considered, it is a veil that both conceals and reveals.

<u>Vedanta, Tantra, and Direct Path.</u> We said above that no people are left without (divine) guidance. The ancient wisdom of central Asia and the Indian sub-continent are instances of that. Fundamentally, what we are concerned with is unitive seeing, this is to say with relating with the world from a centered place—from a "place" of presence, centered within the heart.[150] In what Cynthia Bourgeault has called "one of the most extraordinary sentences ever penned," Jacob Boehme, in the early 17th century, wrote: "For so the eternal delight becomes perceivable, and this perceiving of the Unity is called love."[151] To love anyone or anything is to see that person or thing in the largest possible context.[152]

This is coming to be understood as the most useful background for understanding the life and significance of Jesus Christ and his timeless gift to the world. In the spiritual cultures connected in some way with the Indian sub-continent, there is the language of the chakras that provides a means for considering the human reality. The chakras are best understood as centers of intelligence that constitute the human embodiment.[153]

---

[150] See Robert Sardello, *Heartfulness* (La Veta, Colorado: Goldenstone Press, 2017). See also Cynthia Bourgeault, *Eye of the Heart*, previously cited.

[151] Cynthia Bourgeault, *The Holy Trinity and the Law of Three: Discovering the Radical Truth at the Heart of Christianity* (Boston, Massachusetts: Shambhala Publications, 2013), p. 100, quoting from Boehme's *The Clavis*, facsimile edition (Whitefish, Montana: Kessinger Publishing Company, no date), pp. 22-23.

[152] This is one of the implicit meanings of the expression, "One Love," associated with Rastafari culture. This culture is discussed, in a limited way, further below in Section 7.

[153] In Christian tradition one finds an analogous system in the language of "magnetic center" or centers within the human being. This language can be found in writings of Saint Theophan the Recluse (d. 1894) and deployed at some length in Boris Mouravieff's three-volume, *Gnosis: Study and Commentaries on the Esoteric Tradition of Eastern Orthodoxy*. It is also reflected in the Fourth Way anthropology associated with G. I. Gurdjieff, P. D. Ouspensky, and the psychoanalyst, Maurice Nicoll.

This background also helps us evaluate and critique modern assumptions reflected in the work of popular figures such as (some readings of) the Jesuit anthropologist, Teilhard de Chardin (d. 1955). Among the modern assumptions that are in this way contested is the view that life originates from some complexification of matter.[154] The traditional view of *omne vivum ex vivo* ("life comes from life") that predominates in Indian spiritual cultures is consistent with the *panzoism* that I have previously argued as characteristic of Bulgakovian sophiology.[155]

What is most often meant by the term "Vedanta" in the English-speaking world is the recognition of the importance of non-duality in spiritual accounts of the unfolding of reality within the cosmos.[156] Within this general understanding there is great variation as, for example, descriptions of the phenomenal world as illusory or as real.[157] Sometimes the term "Neo-Vedanta" is used in reference to "qualified non-duality" or the view that, with the Oneness, there is nevertheless

---

[154] Those enamored of the metaphysics of Teilhard are encouraged to explore with equal attentiveness the metaphysics of the Christian philosopher, Beatrice Bruteau (d. 2014), who worked in the field of interspirituality and contemplative thought. With regard to the question of evolution, see a nuanced presentation by Douglas Staley *et al* in a study paper at the website, *Gurdjieff and the Fourth Way: A Critical Appraisal*, on-line at: <http://www. gurdjiefffourthway.org/pdf/EVOLUTION.pdf> (Accessed 8/4/2020).

[155] See Robert F. Thompson, *From Glory to Glory: The Sophianic Vision of Fr. Sergius Bulgakov*, previously cited. The range of meanings of the term, *panzoism*, overlaps with the meanings of the terms, *pansychism* and *hylozoism*. As used in some modern Russian religions writing, *panzoism* signifies a monism of (deathless) life. In Trinitarian context, *panzoism* associates or conjoins with participatory and *panentheist* cosmology. *Panzoism* is similar to *animism* but is not *polytheist* in a classic sense of that word (*polytheism*).

[156] The words, "unfolding of reality," bring to mind the conceptuality of implicate and explicate orders in the work of David Bohm. It was Bohm's insight that in listening to music, for example, one is directly perceiving an implicate order. (Lee Nichol, editor, *The Essential David Bohm*. London: Routledge / Taylor & Francis e-Library, 2005, p. 107.)

[157] This ambiguity of meaning is a reason why some spiritual teachers, such as Adyashanti, have been reserved in their use of the term. Cynthia Bourgeault has preferred the term "unitive seeing" as a way of indicating a meaning without implying a metaphysics. The term non-duality is, of course, a perfectly good term but it requires some discussion of the intended implications.

difference. With regard to a possible Christian Vedanta, the life and work of Fr. Bede Griffiths and the community around him in India come to mind.[158] Beatrice Bruteau is also an important resource for what we may call Christian Vedanta.[159] Fr. Cyprian Consiglio, Prior of the Camaldolese monastery in Big Sur, California, wrote of Fr. Bede Griffiths—and of his outlook, generally—in this way:

> What this all meant[160] furthermore to Bede was that the monk seeks God not through something else, but seeks God directly. Ultimately, the monk does not seek God through work, nor through music, nor through art, nor through study, nor even through service, but through a pure and simple search for a direct, immediate experience of God. This does not necessarily mean that the monk does not work—even the work of evangelization—but somehow the work comes through and from the experience of God, not the other way around. Perhaps ultimately a monk would not so much say, "I find God through music," "I find God through my work," or "I find God through my study," as say "I find music through God, I find study through God, I find work through God." "Let them prefer nothing to the love of God." A monk teacher of mine told me something similar years ago in regards to sacred music, for example; he said he did not think that liturgical music was so much the sound of our searching for God as it was the sound of our having been found by God. It's a subtle dif-ference, but very important. God alone, nothing preferred to the love of Christ.[161]

---

[158] See Wayne Teasdale, *Bede Griffiths: An Introduction to His Interspiritual Thought* (Woodstock, Vermont: SkyLight Paths Publishing, 2003).

[159] See also Swami Chidbrahmananda ("Swami C"), "Vedic Christianity," undated essay at *Vedic Muse* blog. On-line at: <http://vedicmuse.org/wp-content/uploads/2019/09/new-vedic-christianity.pdf> (Accessed 10/5/2020)

[160] This is a reference to the understanding of monasticism as a charism, not primarily as structures. In this connection, Fr. Cyprian had recalled Emanuele Bargellini, Prior General of the Camaldolese, as having said that "monasticism is not a container; it is an energy." There is discussion of monasticism further below at Section 8 of this present text.

[161] From an untitled article by Cyprian Consiglio at his website, July 11, 2005. On-line at: <http://www.cyprianconsiglio.com/5533> (Accessed

It will be useful to recall this notion of seeking God directly, not through something else, in connection with the discussion of "Direct Path" further below in this section.

As briefly noted in an earlier section above (Section 3, "The Imaginarium"), the mandalic structural form derives from traditions known collectively as Tantra, which may have Hindu or Buddhist expressions as well as (earlier) Shaivist expressions. Tantric tradition, including its expression in the practice of yoga, is concerned with energetics. Thomas Matus has pointed out that Tantrism deals more with values than with substances, with process rather than static structure, with relations rather than essences. Matus has also noted that tantric speculation and practice are dominated by the dynamic between the "gross" and the "subtle."[162] This is the cultivation of discernment, a capability that is essential to growth in the spiritual life. Movement in space is energetic. This energy arises from the separation and convergence of the pairs of opposites in the universe. Within the tantras (tantric texts), this implied "energic metaphysics" also links the sounds of words with the ground of reality, which is vibratory energy, *spanda*.[163] It is this energy that works through the imaginal and that manifests in reverie, as that "place" where opposites begin their journey toward reconciliation.[164] Echoing the Argentinian writer, Jorge Luis Borges, it was Terrence McKenna's insight that "scattered through the ordinary world there are books and artifacts and perhaps people who are like doorways into impossible realms, of impossible and contradictory truth."[165] Reverie may begin from unhurried attention to any person or object whatsoever.

What is most interesting to me now, after some years of attention to spiritual traditions associated with Central Asia and the Indian sub-

---

12/7/2020). Note, also, the importance of music in these remarks by Fr. Cyprian.

[162] Matus, *op. cit.*, p. 22.

[163] Matus, *op. cit.*, pp. 37, 40.

[164] We might fruitfully make connection here with the tradition of "bridal chamber" (*hieros gamos*) mysticism, wherein there is "marriage" of the masculine and the feminine.

[165] The quotation appears in an essay by John Horgan, "Was Psychedelic Guru Terence McKenna Goofing About 2012 Prophecy?," *Scientific American* blog, June 6, 2012. On-line at: <https://blogs.scientificamerican.com/cross-check/was-psychedelic-guru-terence-mckenna-goofing-about-2012-prophecy/> (Accessed 11/22/2020)

continent, is what has come to be called, in the English-speaking world, Direct Path. This is, I believe, an awakening to all that is implied in the Judeo-Christian understanding of humanity as created in the image of God. Broadly understood, the Direct Path of spiritual realization is based on the truth of direct (unmediated) connection with the divine life. It therefore honors the revelations preserved within religious traditions, but it does not depend upon them. Two individuals that we might point to as illustrative of this realization are Rumi (d. 1273) and Kabir (15th century).[166] Both of these individuals were embedded within the religious cultures and expectations of their times, but transcended those cultures and expectations. They transcended the temptation to identification with the prevailing religious cultures. When others similarly resist this temptation, their spirituality can also be referred to as Direct Path. A narrower usage of the term "Direct Path" is reflected in the following description as it might be understood by scholars of new religions:

> The Direct Path is the name given to the teaching of Atmananda Krishna Menon and Ramana Maharshi which was brought to the West by Jean Klein. Present-day Direct Path teachers include Francis Lucille, Greg Goode and Rupert Spira. The Direct Path works quite differently from progressive paths as it starts right away with a simple process of self-enquiry that leads directly to the experiential understanding of our true nature as unlimited, unlocated and ever-present Awareness. This initial step (sometimes known as enlightenment) is followed by a much longer stabilization process in which this understanding gradually permeates the way we think, feel, sense the body, perceive the world and relate to others (who are no longer seen as 'others'). Nowadays the Direct Path is regarded by many as a more efficient route to Self-realization than the

---

[166] With regard to Rumi, there are differences of opinion among contemporary scholars about the degree to which Rumi was, or was not, Muslim. In support of the suggestion that Rumi transcended the prevailing spiritual culture, see Mostafa Vaziri, *Rumi and Shams' Silent Rebellion: Parallels with Vedanta, Buddhism, and Shaivism* (New York: Palgrave Macmillan, 2015). There are similar differences of opinion about the character of Kabir's religious identity. For reliable contemporary scholarship on Kabir, see the published work of Charlotte Vaudeville (d. 2006) and Linda Hess.

traditional, progressive paths and one that fits well with a 21st century culture and lifestyle. … There is nothing in the Direct Path teaching that suggests that any preparation is essential although many of those who come to the Direct Path have previously followed a progressive path[167] or spiritual practices of some kind.[168]

The term "Direct Path" as it is used, for example, by Andrew Harvey and others reflects a broader usage.[169] It is characteristic of Direct Path, as Andrew Harvey presents it, to include concern with the bringing into awareness and into manifestation the divine humanity.[170] It can also be noted that spiritual practices are not always experienced as helpful. This understanding appears in some expressions of Carmelite spirituality.[171]

Spiritual practices are meant to serve an awakening that has several aspects. One of these aspects is an awareness that there are degrees or levels of reality. The present moment, for example, exhibits for us reality at its most intense manifestation. Another of these aspects is an awareness that the recounting of "what happened" in history is only

---

[167] The reference to "progressive path" is a reference to the view that there are "steps" (or a "staircase") in the process of enlightenment. What is called Fourth Way "work" (associated with the names of G. I. Gurdjieff, P. D. Ouspensky, Boris Mouravieff, and Maurice Nicoll) tends to stress the need for guidance through stages (away from A and B "influences," toward C influences) on the Way towards Self-realization. See Rebecca Nottingham, *The Work: Esotericism and Christian Psychology* (Independently published, 2018).

[168] From the essay, "Progressive and Direct Paths," at the *Ouspensky Today* website. On-line at: <https://www.ouspenskytoday.org/wp/about-courses/progressive-and-direct-paths/> (Accessed 7/11/2020) . See also Jenny Beal, "The Direct Path to Happiness" (2016), at the same website, on-line at: <https://www.ouspenskytoday.org/wp/wp-content/uploads/The-Direct-Path-to-Happiness.pdf> (Accessed 8/4/2020).

[169] See Andrew Harvey, *The Direct Path: Creating a Personal Journey to the Divine Using the World's Spiritual Traditions* (New York: Broadway Books, 2000).

[170] The divine-humanity appears as a theme throughout all of my previous books, beginning with the first book, *From Glory to Glory* (2016), which is concerned with the sophiology of Fr. Sergius Bulgakov.

[171] See, for example, the introductory discussion in St. John of the Cross, *The Dark Night of the Soul,* translated and introduced by Mirabai Starr (New York: Riverhead Books, 2002).

relatively useful to our central tasks as incarnate beings.[172] Recounting old animosities, true though the story is, in some delimited sense, is not always helpful now, going into the future.

Spiritual practice is also about loosening the hold that our acquired identities have upon us. Spiritual practice provides us with pointers to our highest, deepest, and truest identity. It is also about learning to be comfortable with our growth into cultural hybridity.[173] Who are "my people"? My people are those who are welcoming the light. Following is an example.

<u>The Hyperboean light.</u> We made reference above, at the beginning of this section, to Hyperborea. In a mythological sense, the term references generally northern regions of the planet. The term also refers to a particular quality of light (and life) associated with these northerly regions. The Hyperborean light can be thought of as conducing to great clarity. All things are seen as they are within the divine life. Within the Hyperborean light, vision is limitless and there is no awareness of boundaries. A literary instance of this expansive awareness can be found in the description that Fr. Sergius Bulgakov (d. 1944) gave concerning his first encounter with Sophia. The encounter with Sophia happened in the Caucasus in 1895:

> I was twenty-four years old. For a decade I had lived without faith and, after stormy doubts, a religious emptiness reigned in my soul. One evening, we were driving across the southern steppes of Russia. The strong scented spring grass was gilded by the rays of a glorious sunset. Far in the distance, I saw the blue outlines of the Caucasus. This was my first sign of the mountains. I gazed with ecstatic delight at their rising slopes. I

---

[172] Psychotherapist and Dante scholar, Mark Vernon, has pointed out that In Dante, the souls in Hell do not have a present moment; they are fixated on the past or on the future. (This observation was made in a recorded conversation between Mark Vernon and psychologist, John Vervaeke.)

[173] Our empirical self can be understood in various ways. Using the terminology of his teacher, the historian, Edward Cranz, Tom Cheetham, recognizes two senses of the self—an "intensive" self and an "extensive" self. The self is not simply the mind but, when the mind is the object of consideration, Vervaeke draws on the findings of 4E cognitive science to characterize the mind as embodied, embedded, enactive, and extended.

drank in the light and air of the steppes. I listened to the revelation of nature. My soul was used to the dull pain of seeing nature as a lifeless desert and of treating its surface beauty as a deceptive mask. Yet, contrary to my intellectual convictions, I could not be reconciled to nature without God. Suddenly and joyful in that evening hour my soul was stirred. I started to wonder what would happen if the cosmos were not a desert and its beauty not a mask or deception—if nature were not death, but life. [See the reference to *panzoism* elsewhere in this present book. –RT] What if the merciful and loving Father existed, if nature was a vestige of his love and glory, and if the pious feelings of my childhood, when I used to live in his presence, when I loved him and trembled because I was weak—what if all this were true…. O mountains of the Caucasus! I saw your ice sparkling from sea to sea, your snows reddening under the morning dawn, the peaks which pierced the sky, and my soul melted in ecstasy. The first day of creation shone before my eyes. Everything was clear, everything was at peace and full of ringing joy. My heart was ready to break with bliss. There is no life and no death, only one eternal and unmovable now. *Nunc dimittis* rang out in my heart and in nature. And an unexpected feeling rose up and grew within me—the sense of victory over death. At that moment I wanted to die, my soul felt a sweet longing for death in order to melt away joyfully, ecstatically, into that which towered up, sparkled and shone with the beauty of first creation…. And that moment of meeting did not die in my soul, that apocalypse, that wedding feast: the first encounter with Sophia. That of which the mountains spoke to me in their solemn brilliance, I soon recognized again in the shy, gentle, girlish look on different shores and under different mountains….[174]

The term "Hyperborean" does not appear in this account, but the experience, as Fr. Bulgakov records it, has the qualities that are implicit in the term "Hyperborean light" as used in this present text.

To inhabit this light is the experiential meaning of *theosis*. In the literature of classical Greece, courage is sometimes described as a

---

[174] Sergius N. Bulgakov, *Sophia: The Wisdom of God: An Outline of Sophiology*, (Hudson, New York: Lindisfarne Press, 1993), pp. viii-ix.

(mathematical) mean between fear and fool-hardiness. For those who inhabit the Hyperborean light (or who are in a state of *theosis*), however, there is no fear.[175] There is fearlessness. According to medieval Irish legend and historical tradition, Conaire was a High King of Ireland. About him, the Irish writer and philosopher, John Moriarty (d. 2007) wrote:

> ... [A] man emerges from a pre-Celtic tumulus tomb like Newgrange and walks naked toward Tara, carrying the sun-spear in his hand. [...] He is king of both worlds, this world and the Otherworld. He is, very obviously of course, a type of the risen Christ, whose father also, if only iconographically, was a bird. The sun-spear he carries isn't a warrior's spear .... [...] It is the spear of light that enters Newgrange at the winter solstice. Carrying that spear, a spear by which he was himself transformatively killed, he will re-establish his ancient Bird reign in Ireland. To begin with in Ireland. [...] During his Bird reign the waters of Connla's Well will flow again, the healing waters of the Hawk's Well will flow again, and Eriu, Europa and Ecclesia will come home bearing brimming water-jars on their heads.[176]

> Conaire, whose Bird reign will be distinguished, is walking naked to Tara. [...] Conaire isn't only a type of Christ coming forth from the tomb—he is also Plato's Philosopher King coming forth from the cave. Walk on Conaire. [...] It is time to sing,... The friars are coming over the brine and journeying on the sea. They are bringing Second Coming Christianity. They are bringing Upanishads and Sutras and the Tao Te Ching. They are bringing the Mandukya Om. [...] We have a centre that will hold.[177]

> But Conaire keeps on walking. Naked and with a sunspear in his hand, Conaire keeps on walking to Tara. And, whether we

---

[175] "Yea, though I walk through the valley of the shadow of death, I will fear no evil: for thou art with me; thy rod and thy staff they comfort me." (Psalms 23:4, KJV)

[176] Moriarty, *Dreamtime*, p. x.

[177] Ibid., p. xi.

like it or not, whether we accept the challenge in it or not, we will this day hear the screech of axle-iron in Ireland. Hearing that screech, we will know if we are true.[178]

The fearlessness manifests as adamantine concentration. In this Northern light, understood in an imaginal sense, the Christ manifests with qualities of the falcon—adamantine[179] and all-seeing, with fearsome talons.[180] Virtues blossom—the unfolding of Truth, Goodness, and Beauty as a single reality.[181] More broadly, the Hyperborean light is a reference to the uncreated light manifesting in particular cultures whatever their geographic location. Within Anthroposophic tradition, where attention has been given to this reality, Hyperborea associates with an anticipated new Balto-Finno-Slavic culture of Holy Sophia:

> The Hyperborea of the Greek writers, the land of the sun god Apollo, could be found in the network of initiation centers in the North of Europe. This network existed until about 1000 years ago, until the arrival of Roman and Greek Christianity. The Hyperborea of today is in the etheric world. Its centers are the Grail temple Monsalvat; the home of Vidar; the land of Kalevala; and the zatomis of Heavenly Russia (also described as the Invisible City of Kitezh). These centers inspire individuals and groups who search for the Holy Grail, who connect with Vidar in his mission on behalf of the Etheric Christ, who are

---

[178] Ibid., p. 254.

[179] In humankind, this adamantine quality manifests in the crystallization of what Gurdjieff called the "kesdjan" or soul body.

[180] See the exploration of qualities associated with the falcon in "The Windhover," a poem written by Gerard Manley Hopkins in 1877 and published in 1918. Hopkins dedicated his poem "to Christ our Lord." In Russian iconography, the falcon associates with the third century martyr, Saint Tryphon. Information on-line at: <https://russianicons.wordpress.com/tag/falcons/> (Accessed 11/8/2020)

[181] Jesus Christ is the exemplar of the embodiment of Truth, Goodness, and Beauty as a single reality. To appreciate this perspective, see the trilogy of books by the Greek writer and publisher, Efstratios Papanagiotou: *Spiritual Metamorphosis: The Awakening of the Human Heart*, Second Edition (2013), *Divinization: The Hidden Teaching Within Divine Wisdom*, Second Edition (2013), and *Inner Restoration of Christianity*, Second Edition (2013). All are published by Theosis Books. I suggest they be read in this order.

building the new sampo, and who search for Heavenly Russia by preparing the new Sophianic culture. More generally we may call this the new Balto-Finno-Slavic culture of Holy Sophia. The Hyperborea of the future will be in the land of the 6th culture of Holy Sophia in the Northeast of Europe and, in fact, everywhere where groups of people are connected with her inspirations.... Finland has a special etheric quality of purity that is connected with the powerful forces of nature and its geographical position near or within the Polar Circle. It is exposed to much sunlight in the long days of the summer and to the electro-magnetic field of the sun. In a magical way it carries the memory of the Hyperborean Age when the sun was still connected with the earth.[182]

John Godolphin Bennett (d. 1974) was a British scientist, mathematician, philosopher and author who travelled widely and who integrated scientific research with studies of Asiatic languages and religions. He is particularly well-known for his work with the teachings of Gurdjieff. Here, in brief, is Bennett's view of the Hyperborean source of modern cultures:

The modern world has been produced by the fusion of three great cultures, the Aryan, the Central Asian and the Syro-Egyptian. These cultures have produced three language systems, three basic conceptions of man and God, and three types of society. They have influenced one another, sometimes to the extent of an intimate fusion; but, until the Christian era, they remained recognizably distinct. They can be characterized as the Creator culture, the Spirit culture and the Saviour culture.[183]

---

[182] From Harrie Salman, "The Prophetic *Bylina* and the Russian Mission," in *Starlight: Journal of the Sophia Foundation*, Easter 2020, Volume 20, Number 1, pp. 41-49, pp. 17-48. On-line at: <https://sophiafoundation.org/wp-content/uploads/2020/04/Starlight-Easter-2020-issue-99p.pdf> (Accessed 10/27/2020)

[183] From John G. Bennett's paper, "The Hyperborean Origin of the Indo-European Culture," *Systematics Journal: The Journal of The Institute for the Comparative Study of History, Philosophy and the Sciences*, December 1963, Volume 1, Number 3. See this paper for a much fuller elaboration of the topic. On-

The Hyperborean light is the clear light of Buddha nature. It is both Light and Life. It is the luminosity of all-pervasive life (*panzoism* in the vocabulary of Russian religious thought). The contemporary English sage, John Butler, reflects some awareness of this in his writings and in his teaching of meditation:[184]

No need for anything but this –
Precisely where and what I am
Is life complete – surpassing bliss.
In this alone, all things belong
Where all is right and nothing wrong.

The ability to see the divine fire in all things is a feature of tantric spiritual cultures, including what might be called Christian Tantra. In these cultures, the *mandala* serves as a key organizing principle. As Thomas Matus has noted, within the spiritual cultures of India and surrounding areas, the *mandala* is, in effect, a schematized temple, often in competition with the places of official, brahmanic worship.[185] It is a central and ancient understanding in the Christian way that our human bodies are temples of the Holy Spirit—temples of the divine fire.

<u>Agni Yoga / Surya Yoga.</u> The general orientation that we are commending in this book is a yoga of light. So much is enfolded within that expression—yoga of light! A yoga of light is the natural response to perception of the pervasive and uncreated or divine light. A yoga of light unfolds in all the virtues. There is a theurgic aspect—the uncreated light is deifying. Culturally, a yoga of light unfolds in all the arts and sciences. This yoga of light has ancient roots.[186] This yoga of light is transcends religious boundaries and contexts but, within Christian context, this yoga associates with and identifies with the Christ as source manifestation of Truth, Goodness, and Beauty. For Gurdjieff,

---

line at: <https://www.systematics.org/journal/vol1-3/SJ1-3c.htm> (Accessed 11/4/2020).

[184] For information about John Butler, visit his Spiritual Unfoldment website at: <https://spiritualunfoldment.co.uk/> (Accessed 1/25/2021)

[185] Matus, *op. cit.*, pp. 34-35.

[186] See, for example, Joseph Azize, *The Phoenician Solar Theology An Investigation Into the Phoenician Opinion of the Sun Found in Julian's Hymn to King Helios* (Piscataway, New Jersey: Gorgias Press, 2005).

this mysticism of light entails a practice, a yoga or work on oneself. Joseph Azize, writes:

> Gurdjieff stated that organic life on earth was a process which began in the sun, meaning our visible sun. There is an anecdote that when a chance companion asked Gurdjieff his trade, he replied that he was a salesman of "solar energy." As Gurdjieff died in 1949, this had nothing to do with the commercial exploitation of alternatives to fossil fuels. The human "hero" of *Beelzebub*, is "Ashiata Shiemash," whose name is exactly the Arabic words 'ray of the sun.' Gurdjieff explained his sacred dances by analogy with the sun and planets. Clearly, the sun in Gurdjieff is not an arbitrary metaphor. I contend that just as with the Neoplatonists, Gurdjieff literally believed that the sun possessed a "divine intelligence," that it is the source of either the spiritual faculties themselves (*nous*) or the material which fuels those faculties, and thus a bridge between the human and "divine" worlds.
>
> It must be observed that both Plotinos and Gurdjieff spoke of becoming a sun for oneself. According to Elias the Alexandrian, Plotinus said that "the philosopher must imitate God and the sun and not neglect his body altogether in caring for his soul." Gurdjieff's idea of "creating sun within myself," was described by Adie as: "the experience of an affirmative, positive and intelligent element within myself. This is our aim, this is our doing, to create sun within ourselves."
>
> … [L]ike the Neoplatonists, Gurdjieff was a thinker whose aims, ideas and methods–at least at certain points–include mystical methods. For both the Neoplatonists and Gurdjieff, the sun, and the suns, are critical in the process of the return to the divine. […][187]

In Christian context, the mysticism of solar yoga manifests, for example, in these words from Prayer 16 of *Prayers by the Lake* by Saint Nikolai Velimirović (d. 1956):

---

[187] Joseph Azize, "Solar Mysticism in Gurdjieff and Neoplatonism," previously cited, p. 25.

Indeed, the sun does not know many things as you do, but it does know two things eternally: that it is a servant and a symbol. It knows that it is a servant of the One who kindled it and that it is a symbol of the One who put it at His service.

Be servants of the One who illuminates you with the sun on the outside and with Himself on the inside, and you will taste the sweetness of eternal youth.

Be a symbol of the One who put you among the animals of the earth, and you will surpass the radiance of the sun. Truly all the animals around you will swim in happiness beneath the rays of your goodness, even as moons swim around suns.

Yet what are the sun and all the stars except piles of ashes, through which You shine, O Son of God? Piles of ashes that lessen Your radiance and sift it through themselves like a thick sieve? For indeed, in Your full radiance nothing would be seen except You, just as in total darkness nothing is seen except darkness.

O Lord, Lord, do not scorch us with Your radiance, which is unbearable for our eyes; and do not leave us in the gloom where one grows old and decays.

You alone know the measure of our needs, O Lord, glory to You![188]

Prayer leads into reverie and reverie into prayer. It is significant that the collection of prayers in which the above lines appear is a collection written "by the Lake"—in this instance, Lake Ohrid, one of Europe's deepest and oldest lakes, located in the mountainous border between the southwestern part of North Macedonia and eastern Albania. Poets and saints understand the imaginal power at work in pristine nature, especially natural environments near trees and bodies of water. In the following lines from Prayer 1 of this same collection, consider how continuous is the reality that manifests both as natural world and as divine world:

---

[188] From St. Nikolai of Ochrid and Zica, *Prayers by the Lake*, Prayer 16. Online at: <http://www.sv-luka.org/praylake/index.htm> (Accessed 11/12/2020)

Who is that staring at me through all the stars in heaven and all the creatures on earth?

Cover your eyes, stars and creatures; do not look upon my nakedness. Shame torments me enough through my own eyes.

What is there for you to see? A tree of life that has been reduced to a thorn on the road, that pricks both itself and others. What else—except a heavenly flame immersed in mud, a flame that neither gives light nor goes out?

Plowmen, it is not your plowing that matters but the Lord who watches.

Singers, it is not your singing that matters but the Lord who listens.

Sleepers, it is not your sleeping that matters but the Lord who wakens.

It is not the pools of water in the rocks around the lake that matter but the lake itself.

What is all human time but a wave that moistens the burning sand on the shore, and then regrets that it left the lake, because it has dried up?

O stars and creatures, do not look at me with your eyes but at the Lord. He alone sees. Look at Him and you will see yourselves in your homeland.

What do you see when you look at me? A picture of your exile? A mirror of your fleeting transitoriness?

O Lord, my beautiful veil, embroidered with golden seraphim, drape over my face like a veil over the face of a widow, and collect my tears, in which the sorrow of all Your creatures seethes.

O Lord, my beauty, come and visit me, lest I be ashamed of my nakedness—lest the many thirsty glances that are falling upon me return home thirsty.[189]

This prayer/reverie does not originate in the study or in the chapel. It originates in nature, by the lake. Consider also these words, including reference to the sun, from a poem by English hymn-writer and poet, Dorothy Frances Gurney (d. 1932): "The kiss of the Sun for pardon; the song of the birds for mirth. You are nearer God's heart in a garden than anywhere else on Earth."

---

[189] Ibid., Prayer 1.

Religions are like languages—poetic languages, with great power and delicacy. While we each have a native language, we may—over time—acquire other languages and even obtain some fluency in them. It is the same with religions and their ascetic-mystical and poetic fragrances. It is important to understand that our beliefs are mental crystallizations.[190] They have a function—a role, or a part to play, in our spiritual journey—but, more comprehensively, we become aware of a fragrance. From within a fragrance discerned, there arises a melody. The divine melody gently awakens the sleepers. Consider these lines from the minimalist poet, Robert Lax:

> They lie in slumber late, the acrobats;
> They sleep and do not know the sun is up.
> Nor does the Lord wake them,
> Nor do the sun's rays touch them.
> And the Lord, who has chosen them
> The Lord, who created them,
> Leaves them in slumber until it is time.
> Slowly, slowly, His hand is upon the morning's lyre,
> Makes a music in their sleeping.
> And they turn, and turning wonder
> Eyes awake to light of morning.
> They rise, dismounting from their beds,
> They rise and hear the light airs playing
> Songs of praise unto the Lord.
> The circus is a song of praise,
> A song of praise unto the Lord.
> The acrobats, His chosen people,
> Rejoice forever in His love.[191]

The ancient legend of the Seven Sleepers of Ephesus can be understood as a verbal picture of the subtle divine melody that resurrects children of Adam into a "place" where they see the "unfoldment" of

---

[190] In his "Life of Moses," Saint Gregory of Nyssa (d. c. 395) wrote that concepts are idols. See Paragraph 165 in *Gregory of Nyssa: The Life of Moses*, previously cited, pp. 95-96.
[191] From "The Circus of the Sun" cycle of poems in Robert Lax, *Circus Days and Nights* (New York: The Overlook Press, Peter Mayer Publishers, Inc., 2000).

the life-world they had known before their "falling asleep." In this their brief time of awakening, by divine grace, they see that some things have changed and, alas, some things have not.[192] They see the consequences of actions as unfolded—actions of their own and the actions of others. Stories of this type leave us with an uncanny feeling because we do not discern sequences of causation. What we are presented with are acausal connections—tissues of symbolic relations. The causality at work in this story occurs at another level of reality than our "ordinary" experience of causal relations. This is characteristic of the imaginal realm that manifests in our common world but is not limited to it.[193]

A melody is more complex than a fragrance but it arises from, and seeks to harmonize with, the fragrance. From within the melody arise the hieroglyphs. The written and the spoken words are more complex still and tend toward the utilitarian. In contrast to this tendency, we aspire to remain silent until we are attuned to the fragrance and the melody. Only then will our words, spoken from the heart, accomplish the communion that is the ultimate desire of the divine world for us all, without exception.[194] Listen, with the ear of your heart, to these poetic words from the *Coleccion de Cantares Mexicanos*:

---

[192] See a fuller discussion of the legend of the Seven Sleepers of Ephesus in my book, *The Anthropocosmic Vision*, previously cited. The legend of the Seven Sleepers can be usefully compared with the ancient Irish legend of Saint Mochaoi and the Bird of Heaven. This legend, in a contemporary retelling, can be found in Brendan Ellis Williams, *Seeds from the Wild Verge: Myth, Nature, and Theology in the Border Stream of Celtic Wisdom* (Colorado Springs, Colorado: Ancient Oak Ritual Arts in collaboration with Wandering Words Media, 2020) at pages 226-227.

[193] The Bulgakovian Sophia (Holy Wisdom) is a reality that is operative on both sides of the created/uncreated divide. The imaginal—or at least a certain understanding of it—is analogous to, if not the identical to Sophia in her ways of working to awaken and to enliven all that exists.

[194] Readers might recall the thrust of Whitley Strieber's book, *Communion: A True Story* (New York: HarperCollins / William Morrow Paperbacks, reprint edition, 2008), a *New York Times* non-fiction best seller following its initial publication in 1987.

Destined is my heart to vanish
like the ever withering flowers?
What can my heart do?
At least flowers, at least songs!

My flowers shall not cease to live;
my songs shall never end:
I, a singer, intone them;
they become scattered, they are spread about.

Now do I hear the very words of the *coyolli* bird
as he makes answer to the Giver of Life.
He goes his way singing, offering flowers.
Is that what pleases the Giver of Life?
Is that the only truth on earth?

Eagerly does my heart yearn for flowers;
I suffer with songs, yet I create them on earth,
I, Cuacuauhtzin:
I crave flowers that will not perish in my hands!
Where might I find lovely flowers, lovely songs?
Such as I seek, spring does not produce on earth;
indeed, I feel tormented, I, Cuacuauhtzin.
Perchance, will our friends be happy; will they feel pleasure?
Where might I, Cuacuauhtzin, find lovely flowers, lovely songs?
Our priests, I ask of you:
From whence come the flowers that enrapture man?
The songs that intoxicate, the lovely songs?

Only from His home do they come, from the innermost part of
heaven,
only from there comes the myriad of flowers....
Where the nectar of the flowers is found
the fragrant beauty of the flower is refined....
They interlace, they interweave;
among them sings, among them warbles the *quetzal* bird.[195]

---

[195] These poetic lines from the Nahuatl language are reproduced in a resource
for "Prehispanic Civilizations of Middle America" in the Arizona State
University academic domain. On-line at: <http://www.public.asu.edu/

If there is a philosophy implicit in these beautiful images it can be taken as response or answer to the conditions of limitation arising from humankind's double origin.[196] The attentive reader may have noticed the appearances of "flowers" in the lines above. There is a Sufi proverb that says, "When the flower blossoms, the bees will come." Bees associate with a particular kind of wisdom—the sophianic wisdom that effects ascension (or *theosis*). We will have more to say about that further below.[197]

It is not often acknowledged but elements—or at least fragrances—of the spiritual cultures of Central Asia and the Indian sub-continent, as well as pre-Columbian Mesoamerica, have also found their way into the spiritual culture that has become known as Rastafari. In Lurianic Kabbalah, there is a process of *tikkun* that functions to reconnect all things back to the divine world from which they have fallen. Humankind are invited to assist in that process. Similarly, in Rastafari culture there is a process of *livity*, which is the enlivening of all living things by the one divine life—the One Love. Humankind are invited to assist in this process as well. Both processes contribute to the "ascent" of the created world. More generally, whether one "ascends" by practices of Jewish *merkabah* mysticism or by shamanic practices or whether one "descends" by iatromantic practices, the intent is the same—the healing of whatever or whoever may be in need of it. Reverie as a similar process is in service to creativity and general wellbeing. In the following section we attend to certain aspects of Rastafari culture as a creative response to the slavery of Babylon.

~kitsacat/poetry.html> (Accessed 8/22/2020). The further source, with commentary, for these poetic lines is Chapter III in Miguel Leon-Portilla, *Aztec Thought and Culture: A Study of the Ancient Nahuatl Mind*, revised edition, translated by Jack Emory Davis (Norman, Oklahoma: University of Oklahoma Press, 1963), pp. 76-79. Cuacuauhtzin (d. 1443) was an Aztec poet and warrior.

[196] For insight into the psychospiritual function of doubleness, see psycho-therapist John Welwood's essay, "Double Vision: Duality and Nonduality in Human Experience." On-line at: <http://www.johnwelwood.com/articles/DoubleVision.pdf> (Accessed 9/22/2020). See also footnote 59, page 39, above, in this present text.

[197] At Section 8, "Monasticisms and Indigenization." The association of honey bees with the perennial wisdom is also discussed in my previous book, *Life-Giving Spring: The Eternal Fountain*, a Perennials Study Group publication, Memphis, Tennessee (Kindle Direct Publishing, 2020).

7.   Rastafari and the Light of Ethiopia

Whoever feels it, knows it
… and I feel it, and I know it.[198]

Rastafari, seen from a certain point of view, is an instance of imaginative response—in liminal conditions of life "on the edge"—to the beauty of divine wisdom.   Current issues of racism and wealth inequality as reflected in the "Black Lives Matter" movement all contribute to life on the edge in our time, especially for people of color. Rastafari is, in terms of this present book, an "imaginary" among others.[199]   For those drawn to it, Rastafari can be understood as alternative poetic path to hope and healing.[200]   It is an imaginary formed up from feeding on the Christian scriptures while, at the same time, honoring indigenous roots.   As the Greek philosopher and author, Stelios Ramfos, has pointed out, the Christian scriptures reflect

---

[198] Variation on a traditional Rasta saying. Similar lines can be found in the lyrics to "He Who Feels It Knows It," a song by Bob Marley and the Wailers. The song was released in 1966 and sung by Bunny Wailer. It was re-recorded in 1977 by Bunny Wailer. The lyrics can be found on-line at: <https:// www.jah-lyrics.com/song/bob-marley-the-wailers-he-who-feels-it-knows-it> (Accessed 7/2/2020)

[199] A four-point typology (orthodox-isolated, orthodox-integrated, secular-spiritual, secular-cultural) has been suggested as a means of establishing an applicable vocabulary with which various phenomena of Rastafari expression can be considered, while at the same time recognizing the authenticity of contrasting expressions. This typology was proposed by K. Gandhar Chakravarty (University of KwaZulu-Natal, South Africa) in an article, "Rastafari Revisited: A Four-Point Orthodox/Secular Typology," *Journal of the American Academy of Religion*, March 2015, Volume 83, Issue 1, pp. 151–180. On-line at: <https://doi.org/10.1093/jaarel/lfu084> (Accessed 7/25/2020)

[200] To borrow words from the title of Brenda Domínguez-Rosado's book, *Sufism as Lorna Goodison's Alternative Poetic Path to Hope and Healing* (Newcastle upon Tyne, U.K.: Cambridge Scholars Publishing, 2019). Lorna Goodison, as previously mentioned, is a Jamaican poet. Brenda Domínguez-Rosado is a tenured professor of English at the University of Puerto Rico.

diverse perspectives on Jesus. With regard to the New Testament, he writes:

> Its twenty-seven books tell of the matters "in many ways" and thus we encounter tensions, such as between John and the three other Evangelists, or even clear disagreements, such as between Paul and James. At the same time there is a constant point of reference—the recognition of the fact of human salvation in the person of Jesus Christ, the confession of faith in his crucifixion and resurrection. The concept of salvation now goes beyond the Old Testament sense of escape from deadly dangers to cover the fears and anxieties that, as a spiritual threat, accompany the human insistence on self-justification.[201]

Given that fact of diverse perspectives, it ought not to be surprising that meditation upon these scriptures give rise to divergent understandings which, in the Kingdom, are in harmony and at peace with each other even as they are different. Rastafari is one such understanding. What is called "the Kingdom" is another name for the divine Wisdom stream.

Who are the Rastafari and how might we characterize them? In attempting to understand any culture that seems in any way or in some way "different," it is useful to utilize both insider and outsider perspectives because these together have a hand in shaping the creatively imagined entity under consideration.[202] According to one understanding, Rastafari culture can be regarded as a contemporary expression of Essene spirituality.[203] Rastafari can also be viewed as a mystery school (within the wisdom stream of ancient Egypt, broadly

---

[201] Stelios Ramfos, "The Secret Jesus," an English translation, p. 9. On-line at: <https://www.academia.edu/24236489/THE_JESUS_SECRET> (Accessed 6/25/2020)

[202] This method of using both insider and outsider perspectives is on effective display in Alexander D. Knysh's substantive book, *Sufism: A New History of Islamic Mysticism* (Princeton, New Jersey: Princeton University Press, 2017).

[203] See, for example, Abba Yahudah Berhan Sellassie, *A Journey to the Roots of Rastafari: The Essene Nazarite Link*, edited by Vik Slen (Emeryville, California: WordSword Publishing, 2013).

considered).[204] What is called "Christian Tantra" is a similar expression of conscious transmission of primordial wisdom. In the West, the primordial wisdom is fundamentally a certain type of Platonism within which there is a unity of the virtues that, together, comprise the Beautiful. In this context Classical and early Christian learning (*paideia*) in the West was oriented toward this end. This is the root, in the West, of the primordial wisdom. This particular Platonic stream is the fountainhead source of the mystical dimensions of the Abrahamic religions—Judaism (Kabbalah), Christianity (Hesychasm), and Islam (Sufism). Connected with these understandings is a yet further insight having to do with the East.[205] This is the insight that Christianity, Islam, and Buddhism are three dimensions of a single revelation.[206]

<u>Invitation to sovereignty.</u> In the folklore of the West Indies and in Rastafari storytelling there is a spider figure—Anancy—that, with hidden and malevolent motives, approaches people with insinuating words:

> Anancy is a petty hustler and a schemer. He became an artist at psychological warfare, a tireless weaver, a trickster, a master of disguise and intrigue, a con-artist with his words, his tongue and his body movements. He constantly "works his brains" to further his schemes and is thus dubbed a "jinnal," a "scamp," a "rascal" or a "samfie-man." As a tactician he is indirect and circular. Even when he looks you in the eye it is merely an

---

[204] See Chapter 2, "Rastafari–Ancient Mystic Foundations," in Dennis Forsythe, *Rastafari: For the Healing of the Nations* (New York: One Drop Books, 1999). This perspective is also reflected in Tyson Brown, *Abba Keddus: Rastafari and the Return of Our Sacred Origins* (Morrisville, North Carolina: Lulu.com, 2011).

[205] For an account of how the primordial wisdom in the East made connection with the West, see Peter Kingsley, *A Story Waiting to Pierce You: Mongolia, Tibet and the Destiny of the Western World* (Point Reyes, California: Golden Sufi Center Publishing, 2010). For levels of intentionality that may be at work in cultural connections, see also Ernest Scott, *The People of the Secret* (London: Octagon Press, 1985).

[206] This is similar to the notion elaborated in Jean-Yves Leloup, *Judas and Jesus: Two Faces of a Single Revelation*, previously cited, that the reality and story of the Apostle Judas and of Jesus Christ together constitute dimensions of a single revelation.

outward sham. He is a natural actor and dramatist who loves
to be noticed. He believes in style and class and on the whole
possesses a charmed life. You can never know his mind, for he
is always up to some trick and always twisting his mouth and
lying in the name of truth. He is an extrovert, more concerned
with impressing others. You can never take what he says
seriously; even when he laughs or agrees with you, you know it
can be a trick or game calculated to achieve his particular goal,
as he conceives it and which usually amounts to his getting a
little bit more for himself and for his family or his tribe, from
the system which overpowered him.[207]

In Rastafari spiritual culture, there is inculcated as desirable the growth
in character from spider (Anancy) to lion—and from lion to lamb.
Dennis Forsythe discusses this progression at some length:

> The straight and narrow path out of Anancism (for Anancy) is
> the path of the Lion, say the majority of Rastafarians. They
> strive, therefore, to become lion-men.
>
> [...]
>
> Rastas start off as Anancies, but for Jah-related reasons they
> reincarnate themselves in and through the image of the dreaded
> African lion which they see as a more fitting Rasta ideal of
> Black manhood, expressing more of the natural and ideal spirit
> of Africans and offering a more wholesome definition of how
> they should live socially and feel inwardly. The lion thus repre-
> sents the Brethren's symbolic yearning for power and whole-
> someness to compensate for their powerlessness and their
> alienated existence. It symbolizes the resurgence of ancient
> African vibrations, ideals and definition of self. The lion sym-
> bolizes his own first person image of himself, as he transforms
> himself by discovering the secrets of getting more power.[208]

Lion-man is not, however, the pinnacle of character development in
Rastafari spiritual culture. Continuing spiritual unfoldment of the
human reveals the lamb-man:

---

[207] Forsythe, *Rastafari*, p. 107.
[208] Forsythe, p. 111, pp. 113-114.

"Many are called, but few are chosen."

While the majority of Rastafarians identify themselves with the dreaded lion, it does come through their overall movements and symbolisms that there is yet a higher level that is possible: that of the lamb.

In Eastern philosophy, this lamb-level is defined in numerical symbolism as the seventh level of consciousness, an internal clairvoyance stage in which one clearly sees and comprehends everything through infinite time and space, and manifesting itself as universal love and the capacity to embrace all opposites and turn them into complements.

[...]

Rastafarians are very conscious of differing levels of movements, of "ranking" and of "heights." The Lamb rank or "heights" is a measure of how far the lion-man has traveled out of the bottomless pit (of Babylon). At this level, he is qualitatively changed in the direction of greater spiritual awareness and power. There is de-emphasis on outward symbols and rituals, including locks and herbal smoking, which were so important in his initial movements. The more certain he becomes of his own mental liberation, the more certain he rises to the spiritual heights of the lamb. At this level he might even forego his locks without feeling devitalized.[209]

This progression from lion-man to lamb-man is inspired, at least partly, by spiritual currents from Ethiopian Orthodox Christianity. Without that Christian element or contribution there is a tendency for personal development to stop prematurely at the level of lion-man. It may be that within Ethiopian Orthodox spiritual psychology, however, the lion itself has become equivalent to the Rasta lamb. Another symbolic equivalence is the species of herb that is called "lambsbread," bringing to mind the Bread of the Lamb in Orthodox Christian symbology.[210]

---

[209] Forsythe, pp. 115, 121.

[210] In her book, *Eye of the Heart: A Spiritual Journey into the Imaginal*, previously cited, Cynthia Bourgeault calls attention to Logion 7 of the Gospel of Thomas: "Blessed is the lion whom the man devours, for that lion will become man. But cursed is the man whom the lion devours, for that lion will become man." Clearly, the lion state is not the highest state of humanization.

This unfolding within awareness of the human *telos*, the "high calling" of humankind is the invitation to sovereignty, understood in a certain way:

Yeshua says …
If you are searching, you must not stop until you find.
When you find, however, you will become troubled.
Your confusion will give way to wonder.
In wonder you will reign over all things.
Your *sovereignty* will be your rest.[211]
— Logion 2, *The Gospel of Thomas*

<u>The King of Kings / The God-Man.</u> The notion of sovereignty goes all the way up, as it were—that is to say that true sovereignty is a divine attribute that never loses its connection with the divine, even when manifested in the temporal world. It is characteristic of Rastafari "overstanding" that Emperor Haile Selassie I of Ethiopia (crowned, November 2, 1930) is a Messianic figure. There is, however, a diversity of opinion within Rastafari communities about the meanings and implications of holding the Emperor in this high regard.[212]

It is good, at this juncture, to recall the centrality of the notion of God-manhood in modern Russian religious thought. The religious philosopher, Nicholas Berdyaev, for example, wrote: "Both philosophy and theology should start neither with God nor with man, but rather with the God-man. The basic and original phenomenon of life is the meeting and interaction of God and man, the movement of God towards man and of man towards God."[213] In Rasta culture, Selassie I

---

[211] *The Luminous Gospels*, p. 9. On the topic of "wonder," see Bishop Seraphim Sigrist's delightful book, *Theology of Wonder* (Crestwood, New York: St. Vladimir's Seminary Press, 1999).

[212] For extensive discussion of this topic see William David Spencer, *Dread Jesus* (Eugene, Oregon: Wipf and Stock, 2011). The association of Emperor Haile Selassie I of Ethiopia with the Christ is not unique. Within spiritual cultures of India one also recognizes manifestations of the god-man in, for example, Sai Baba of Shirdi (d. 1918), Sathya Sai Baba (d. 2011), and the semi-legendary Mahavatar Babaji.

[213] From Nicholas Berdyaev, *Freedom and the Spirit,* as quoted in Evgueny Lampert, *Nicolas Berdyaev and the New Middle Ages* (London: James Clarke & Co., Ltd., [1945]), p. 33. This blends with what is said elsewhere in this present text about the dual origins of humankind.

is regarded as an *icon* of Christ. May it be so for each of us as well! "People see His Majesty not only as a human being, but also an angel. He was the light of Ethiopia… It is also told that His Majesty was born according to a prophecy."[214] Norman Hugh Redington provides an early assessment of the Rastafari movement from the perspective of an Orthodox Christian:

> I believe that the Rastafarians have been greatly underestimated by the outside world, including, to some extent, many elements in the Orthodox community. The classical Rastas were sophisticated theological and philosophical thinkers, not cargo-cultists worshiping newspaper photos of an African despot. They had discovered many sophisticated theological concepts for themselves, and had retraced many of the Christological and other debates of the early Church. They brought a truly rich cultural and artistic legacy, including some of the twentieth century's most moving hymnography.[215]

Rastafari is improvisation in a spiritual key—it is Word-Sound-Power, a triadic concept suggesting that the "I and I vibration" of speech and music impact the world, both physically and socially. If Rastafari, as a sociological phenomenon, is not aboriginal in its Caribbean and North American history, it does appear to be an attempt to reconnect with the aboriginal wisdom in an Ethiopian Christian epigenetic[216] sense and shape. It is a creative attempt to re-indigenize the ancient wisdom in resistance to, and subversion of, the machinery of the Babylon system. As indigenous cultures live in perpetual reverie, their language has a poetic quality to it. In Rastafari culture it is just this that passes through the defense mechanisms of Babylon. Rastafari is not only about leaving Babylon—Bob Marley's album, *Exodus*, comes to

---

[214] As quoted in article by Ras Red Lion, "Birth of the Redeemer: Emperor Haile Selassie I," July 19, 2019, at the Rastafari Coalition website. On-line at: <https://www.rastafaricoalition.org/articles/redeemer.htm> (Accessed 10/16/2020)

[215] Norman Hugh Redington, "A Sketch of Rastafari History," The Saint Pachomius Library, 1995. On-line at: <http://www.voskrese.info/spl/rasta-hist.html> (Accessed 7/3/2020)

[216] The term, "epigenetic," is a reference to some quality or characteristic relating to, or arising from, non-genetic influences on gene expression.

mind—it is also about searching for Zion. The bi-racial writer, Emily Raboteau, has understood Zion as a metaphor for freedom, a spiritual realm rather than a geographical one—and yet she has recognized that people that have risked everything in search of a "promised land," a territory that is hard to define and harder to inhabit.[217]

The use of cannabis in Rastafari communal settings also serves the purpose of evading the mechanisms of the Babylon system. As with other entheogens in other social and spiritual contexts, cannabis use has the function of pacifying the personal ego, which enables clear seeing of things and situations as they are. Interbeing is revealed. The connections of all things with all things are not illusory, but these connections cannot be clearly discerned when egoic interests skew the phenomena. We have made reference, elsewhere in this present text, to active and passive modes of reverie. Cannabis reveals the energetic and shimmering nature of reverie that is continuous with all of nature and with what we may call supernature. The divine world (supernature) interacts meaningfully with what we may call the empirical or "ordinary" world. This interaction is discerned in the imaginal realm, but there are no parts of the empirical or common realms that are exempt or exterior to the dynamism of the imaginal. This dynamism manifests most clearly in reverie. As we engage with the topic within the pages of this present book, something like a definition begins to form: reverie as the dynamism of meaningful connections revealed over time.

It has been a great gift of Rastafari cultural creativity that it seeks to embody a harmonious and non-exploitative relationship with the natural world. In the following section we attend, more generally, to two aspects of relationship with the natural world—indigenization and those practices of generosity and non-attachment that are today understood as expressions of monastic life. Both indigenous cultures and monastic life have a great deal to teach us about living lightly upon the earth. Paradisal life is the reverie that flows from such ways of living.

---

[217] For the various dimensions and ways of understanding the search, see Emily Raboteau, *Searching for Zion: The Quest for Home in the African Diaspora* (New York: Atlantic Monthly Press, 2013). Raboteau's book contains these words: "As long as there is Babylon, there must be Zion." And, as Professor Darren Middleton (Texas Christian University) has observed elsewhere, as long as there is Zion, there must be Zion singers (Psalms 137:3).

8.   Monasticisms and Indigenization

Beehive

"Monasticism is not a container; it is an energy."[218]
— Emanuele Bargellini OSB Cam

Being witness to paradisal life as opposed to direct resistance to Babylon is one perspective. Another perspective is to be concerned with incarnating the paradisal life as opposed to simply being its witness. Granted the insightfulness of Dom Emanuele Bargellini's pithy observation quoted above, it seems more accurate to say that monasticism has both a container aspect and an energetic aspect. Benedictine life, for example, is designed or shaped in such a way as to provide a kind of "container" for cultivation of the paradisal life, which is characterized by the recognition of "the ordinary" as sacred and light-filled. Monastic communities, especially Benedictine communities, have as an essential purpose the orientation or re-orientation of oneself to life in God. Friars and some monastic communities, Benedictine or otherwise, have external apostolates or missions, but what we may call primitive Benedictine life has the *Opus Dei* (the work of God or liturgical prayer) as the essential centerpiece of its communal life.

Paradisal life is not only for humankind. Consider this telling and insightful remark concerning the forest churches in Ethiopia: "These forests are not just good for people, they are also the last shelter for wild animals. In our tradition, the church is like an ark. A shelter for every kind of creature and plant. If a wildcat or little kudu or vervet monkey leaves the church forest, immediately he will be killed. Here the animals are safe."[219] This is what churches should be and this is

---

[218] These words were spoken to Ciprian Consiglio OSB Cam. On-line at: <http://www.cyprianconsiglio.com/5533> (Accessed 9/11/2020)

[219] This is an observation offered by forest ecologist, Dr. Alemayehu Wassie, as quoted in an undated multimedia essay by Fred Bahnson, "The Church Forests of Ethiopia: A Mystical Geography," *Emergence Magazine* (website).

what monastic life, especially Benedictine life, at its best, is and ought to be.[220]

It is not uncommon in the narrative of Holy Scripture to see uncovered before the reader's eyes the working out of karmic debt. Similarly, we might recall the story of St. Benedict's disheartening decision to cut down the trees of Apollo's sacred grove at Monte Cassino, which might seem—as if it were a replication of the primordial Fall—to somehow foreshadow, as consequences, the unhappy chapters of great suffering in the history of Benedictine (and, more generally, monastic) life in the West. This history records depredation and destruction of communities of light. The downfall of religious communities can be traced, more directly, to the hazards of power and wealth, both within and beyond these communities. With varying degrees of success over the course of its history, Benedictine life has resisted being shaped by, through, and for the benefit of external powers. Within the context of this present book, what is most noteworthy about Benedictine tradition is the rhythmic character of its day-to-day life and its recognition of the value of sustained attention—from the daily office, including psalmody and the reading of scripture to various productions of craft and sacred arts. Within Benedictine tradition learning and theology grow out of *lectio divina*. This is in contrast to "School" (or Scholastic) theology as it developed within the medieval universities. In Benedictine imagery and hagiography, a raven often appears in association with St. Benedict. The raven is said to have carried away a loaf of poisoned bread that a jealous enemy had sent to Benedict. In a wider, mythic, context, ravens are recognized as bringers of light.[221] It seems fitting, therefore, that Benedictine tra-

---

On-line at: <https://emergencemagazine.org/story/the-church-forests-of-ethiopia/> (Accessed 7/24/2020)

[220] Violence, however, has deep roots. For insight into these deep-rooted layers, ponder the songs of the Buddhist teacher, Milarepa, as he separately addresses the deer, the dog, and the hunter, all of whom are caught up in a cycle of fear and violence. In Garma C. C. Chang, translator, *The Hundred Thousand Songs of Milarepa*, reprint edition (New York: Harper Colophon, 1970), pp. 142-153. Also on-line at: <http://www.kreisels.com/milarepa/milarepa-songs-english.htm> (Accessed 9/12/2020)

[221] See the mythological raven story from the Northwestern lands of North America as retold in Williams, *Seeds from the Wild Verge*, previously cited, at pp. 280-281.

dition has been and continues to be associated with a certain kind of knowledge—luminous or illuminating knowledge.

What we discover, however, is that *lectio divina* is not the only feeding practice of its kind. Reverie, as discussed in this present text, concerns the ingestion of the food of impressions. Images (visual impressions, a particular kind of impressions more generally) may serve as occasion for what we may refer to as *visio divina*. This practice leads through contemplation of the image into more conscious awareness of the all-comprehensive divine Presence. This associates with the true function of all art forms. There is also a kinesthetic dimension to all work that incarnates or manifests beauty. This is particularly evident in craft work of all types.[222]

As Vlad Naumescu has pointed out, the novitiate in Eastern Christian monastic tradition is a period of learning to experience the presence of God in one's life and the world. Novices follow the hesychast prayer, a mystical tradition that leads them to an experiential knowledge of God. In that context, the novitiate is regarded as a complex learning process involving specific assemblages of contextual, cognitive, body-sensory and emotional aspects. By educating their attention and emotion, novices learn to see beyond and within reality and thus discover the potentiality of people and things "in the likeness of God." Orientation towards the transcendent requires an expansion of the imaginative capacities beyond their "routine" functioning. Imagination could be thus seen as a key cognitive capacity through which they learn to experience God.[223] Imagination serves to sensitize or shape perception.[224] Benedictines in the West would do well to be aware of this in designing their own novitiate and on-going (continuing) formation programs.

Benedictine life also has cultural implications. As St. Benedict has long been referred to as patron saint of Europe, we might inquire what it is about Benedictine life that might contribute to the future of Europe. Rowan Williams, in an essay on "Benedict and the Future of Europe," focuses on three aspects of the Rule of Benedict: the use of time, and what the Rule has to say about obedience, and what the Rule

---

[222] The sculptor, Eric Gill (d. 1940), for example, is mentioned in footnote 236 at page 114, further below.

[223] Naumescu, *op cit.*

[224] John Vervaeke has recognized in his work this function of the imagination.

has to say about participation.[225] In connection with the use of time, we note the significance of rhythms in Benedictine life. It is these rhythms—in addition to Benedictine life as a "container"—that are perennially useful features. By rhythms we mean the various rhythms of the day, of the week, of the seasons, and of the liturgical year. We might even say the rhythms of a human life. These rhythms harmonize and make possible a spiritual culture of particular fragrance. Benedictine rhythms are not mechanical, but are nested in the larger cosmic rhythms.[226] Additionally, Benedictine life is about the practicalities and, we may say, the poetics of household management. It is this essential characteristic that enables communities—any community—to flourish.

Here in the Western world there is a temptation to over-emphasize the perceived contrast between what we may call Benedictine monastic style with Celtic Christian monastic style. (These can, however, be thought of as, in some respects, directional pointers or tendencies along a continuum.) The argument on behalf of their commonalities has been well-expressed by, among others, the Anglican lay theologian, Esther de Waal.[227] Consider, for example, this beautiful and well-known poem attributed to St. Manchán (d. 664), a monk of Lemanaghan, County Offaly, Ireland:

> I wish, O Son of the living God, O ancient, eternal King,
> For a hidden little hut in the wilderness that it may be my
>   dwelling.
> An all-grey lithe little lark to be by its side,
> A clear pool to wash away sins through the grace of the Holy
>   Spirit,
> Quite near, a beautiful wood around it on every side,
> To nurse many-voiced birds, hiding it with its shelter.

---

[225] The essay appears as Chapter 5 in Rowan Williams, *The Way of St. Benedict*, previously cited.

[226] For insight into the larger scale cosmic rhythms see *Hamlet's Mill: An Essay Investigating the Origins of Human Knowledge and its Transmission Through Myth* (Jaffrey, New Hampshire: David R. Godine, Publisher / Nonpareil Books, 1969, 1977) by Giorgio de Santillana and Hertha von Dechend.

[227] See Esther de Waal's essay, "Where Celtic and Benedictine Traditions Meet," and substantial essays by other authors in Linda Burton and Alex Whitehead, editors, *Christ is the Morning Star: When Celtic Spirituality meets the Benedictine Rule* (Dublin, Ireland: Lindisfarne Books, 1999).

A southern aspect for warmth, a little brook across its floor,
A choice land with many gracious gifts such as be good for
    every plant.
A few men of sense we will tell their number
Humble and obedient. to pray to the King:
Four times three, three times four, fit for every need,
Twice six in the church, both north and south:
Six pairs besides myself
Praying for ever the King who makes the sun shine.
A pleasant church and with the linen altar-cloth, a dwelling for
    God from Heaven;
Then, shining candles above the pure white Scriptures.
One house for all to go to for the care of the body,
Without ribaldry, without boasting, without thought of evil.
This is the husbandry I would take, I would choose, and will
    not hide it:
Fragrant leek, hens, salmon, trout, bees.
Raiment and food enough for me from the King of fair fame,
And I to be sitting for a while praying God in every place.[228]

The love of the natural world that is apparent in this poem is particularly associated with Celtic spirituality, but the emphasis on humility, obedience and simplicity—also in this poem—seems completely consistent with the Benedictine Rule. Elements of balanced Benedictine life—prayer, work and study—can also be found in St. Manchán's poem. The central intent of monastic life, whether it is characterized as Celtic or Benedictine, is the same—the remembrance of God and the continual awareness of the Divine Presence.[229]

At the present time and for the foreseeable future, the way forward for Benedictine and New Monastic communities generally is to become more consciously rooted in the Earth, the natural environment—including the wide diversity of both plant and animal life—and atten-

---

[228] This poem by St. Manchán, as translated here by Kuno Meyer, is also known as "The Hermit's Song."

[229] Dom Alistair Bate OSBA makes these observations about St. Manchán's poem in an essay, "Celtic and Benedictine—Common Ground?" at the website of the Holy Celtic Church International. On-line at: <https:// holycelticchurch.weebly.com/celtic--benedictine.html> (Accessed 9/7/2020)

tive to its care.[230] This is the indigenization that all spiritual communities in our time are being called toward.[231] Spiritual communities are being invited to explore what it means to be inter-dependent with others.[232] To better understand the relations between what can be thought of as Benedictine life and the Celtic stream, consider the image of an English garden. The typically English garden is not completely ordered (as we might imagine a French garden designed along the lines of Versaille), but neither is it completely wild and unattended. The gift of Benedictine life, it seems to me, is the stability and the orderliness with which the most ordinary things in the common life can be done— thus revealing or showing the luminosity of the ordinary. The Celtic stream's great gift is its valuing of wildness, the wildness without which we cannot life an authentically human life.[233]

It has been suggested that, at least in the ancient world, there is something of a paradox in monastic life having to do with the tension between separation from the world and the offering of hospitality and service in it.[234] This paradox, to the extent that it is not just an ancient

---

[230] An important resource for community reflection is the *Earth Charter*. For both text and context, on-line: <https://earthcharter.org/> (Accessed 1/24/2021)

[231] For an important discussion of inter-spiritual indigenization in Ireland, see Bernadette Flanagan and Michael O'Sullivan, "Spirituality in Contemporary Ireland: Manifesting Indigeneity," *Spiritus: A Journal of Christian Spirituality*, Volume 16, Number 2A, Fall 2016, pp. 55-73. On-line at: <https://www. researchgate.net/publication/314241050_Spirituality_in_Contemporary_ Ireland_Manifesting_Indigeneity> (Accessed 9/8/2020)

[232] This inter-dependency is acknowledged and reflected in the Emerging Earth Community network. On-line at: <http://emergingearthcommunity. org/> (Accessed 1/24/2021)

[233] To better appreciate the significance of this gift of wildness, see the work of the Irish philosopher and writer, John Moriarty. <https:// shuindingle.com/john-moriarty-institute/> (Accessed 9/17/2020), and the storyteller, Martin Shaw <https://drmartinshaw.com/> (Accessed 9/17/2020). See also the collection of essays by Brendan Ellis Williams, *Seeds from the Wild Verge*, previously cited.

[234] The suggestion is made by Marlena Whiting (University of Amsterdam) in her paper, "The Monastic Paradox: negotiating monastic seclusion and pilgrim hospitality in the Late Antique Near East" in the academic blog, *Hypotheses*, October 12, 2016. On-line at: <https://hospitam.hypotheses.org/510> (Accessed 9/12/2020)

phenomenon, is perhaps more acute in Benedictine communities at particular times and places in their history. From a psychological perspective, however, it is understood that both of these directionalities are always at work, at the personal level, in any substantial friendships. In therapeutic settings there is also recognition of the risks associated with identification and projection. In the indigenization process, to the extent that we are attentive, we become aware of the loving reality that holds together the foregrounded binaries that attract our attention. This is what is meant by ascension that is never-ending. We are "bees of the invisible." This is how the Bohemian-Austrian poet, Rainer Maria Rilke (d. 1926), characterized our role in the ascension process when he wrote:

> Everywhere transience is plunging into the depths of Being… It is our task to imprint this temporary, perishable earth into ourselves so deeply, so painfully and passionately, *that its essence can rise again, invisible, inside us.* We are the bees of the invisible. We wildly collect the honey of the visible, to store it in the great golden hive of the invisible.[235]

---

[235] Rainer Maria Rilke in a letter to Halewicz, *Duinio Elegies*, from *Letters on Life.* Language adapted and emphasis added—RT. On-line source: <http://www. math.buffalo.edu/~sww/0Gurdjieff/beesoftheinvisibleworld_vol1.pdf> (Accessed 10/1/2020). For more on the deep symbolics of bees, see Neil Rusch, "Honey Song: What the bees—and the Bushmen—know," *Parabola*, Fall 2018, Volume 43, Number 3. On-line at: <https://parabola.org/2018/ 07/28/honey-song-by-neil-rusch/> (Accessed 10/1/2020). See also Martha Heyneman, "Bees of the Invisible World," *Parabola*, Fall 2005, Volume 30, Number 3. In a lecture at Esalen, Brother David Steindl-Rast OSB commented on Rilke as follows: "So, the body for Rilke becomes the place where this transformation takes place. And this is what we start working on from our childhood—only we don't know it; later on we might become aware of it. Every moment we translate the visible, the nectar of the visible, into that golden honeycomb of the invisible." This remark, in the recording of the lecture on the topic of "The Body, Sensuousness and Spirituality" at Esalen, can be found on-line, in Part 2, at about 15 minutes in, at: <https:// gratefulness.org/resource/sensuousness-and-spirituality/> (Accessed 1/10/2021)

While this notion of ascension/resurrection is a theme in the awareness of Nikolai Fedorov (d. 1903) and the Russian cosmists, in particular, it is also a concern of Christian spirituality, more generally.

Benedictine life has always understood the place and value of work in their common life.[236] Work or ascetic practice serves the common task of ascension. This is especially true when the Benedictine community recognizes the profundity or depth of the possibilities inherent in its self-understanding as a "school of the Lord's service."[237] In our time Benedictine and other spiritual communities might again seek to explore traditional crafts as a means toward indigenization in the Earth as interdependent localized communities.

Some readers of this present text may be familiar with Dorothy Day and the Catholic Worker Movement. One of the inspirations for this movement was the French Catholic social activist and theologian, Peter Maurin (d. 1949), whose vision for the movement drew from Benedictine wells.[238] The vision had to do with enabling transformation of the social order. The means toward realization of this vision were the following: The movement would (1) establish urban houses of hospitality to care for the destitute, (2) establish rural farming communities to teach city dwellers agrarianism and encourage a movement back-to-the-land, and (3) set up roundtable discussions in community

---

[236] Eric Gill and the arts and crafts movement associated with William Morris and John Ruskin and others from the late 19th century come to mind. Of particular value for the theoretics of indigenization in our own time is the work of design theorist, Christopher Alexander (University of California, Berkeley), especially in his *Notes on the Synthesis of Form* (1964) and his later writings, including *The Nature of Order* (in four volumes, 2005). Cynthia Bourgeault has characterized Benedictine life as work and prayer (*Ora et Labora*) in terms of a diagram of four quadrants—work (alone and with others) and prayer (alone and with others).

[237] The sense of "school" here, in this instance, includes all that is understood in a Fourth Way sense of "school" (associated with Gurdjieff) as the context for "work" on smoothing out the sharp edges of personalities that can only happen when there is conscious consent to undergo the benefits of interpersonal and situational "friction."

[238] See Mark and Louise Zwick, "Virgil Michel, Benedictine Co-Worker of Dorothy Day and Peter Maurin: Justice embodied in Christ-life and Liturgy," *Houston Catholic Worker*, February 1, 2000. On-line at: <https://cjd.org/2000/02/01/virgil-michel-benedictine-co-worker-of-dorothy-day-and-peter-maurin-justice-embodied-in-christ-life-and-liturgy/> (Accessed 1/9/2021)

centers in order to clarify thought and initiate action.[239] Maurin saw similarities between his approach and what he viewed was that of the Irish monks who evangelized medieval Europe. It may be that New Monastic communities today could revisit these three ideas in discerning a way forward for today.

There is a story that is told about Saint Benedict that encapsulates much of what we are discussing in this present book:

> When the brothers were still asleep, the man of God, Benedict, got up to watch in prayer before the time for the Night Office. Standing at the window and praying to almighty God in the middle of the night, he suddenly saw a light pour down that routed all the shadows. It shone with such splendor that it surpassed daylight, even though it was shining in the darkness. A wonderful thing followed in this vision, for as Benedict reported later, the whole world was brought before his eyes as if collected in a single ray of sunlight.[240]

When reverie unfolds as unified vision in this way ("the whole world … as if collected in a single ray of sunlight"), we experience what is called, in other terminology, the uncreated light. We will reflect on this reality in the following section. These reflections, however, merely touch "the hem of the garment" of the subject of divine illumination and its powerfully transformative effects. Reverie is a dynamism of ascension. It is the dynamic movement toward transcendence of every phenomenal and conceptual binary. It is also the "root work"—the grounding—that subverts every ideology and accepts the ashes and rubble of these crumbling ideologies (towers of Babel).

---

[239] Peter Maurin's Three-Point Program is discussed in his *Easy Essays* (Eugene, Oregon: Wipf and Stock Publishers, 2010; previously published by Rose Hill Books, 2003).

[240] From Terrence G. Kardong, *The Life of St. Benedict by Gregory the Great: Translation and Commentary* (Collegeville, Minnesota: Liturgical Press, 2009), pp. 131-132. For the attentive reader, the expression, "a single ray of sunlight," may bring to mind references elsewhere in this present text to "Ray of Creation" in Gurdjieff's spiritual cosmology.

9. Saint Symeon and the Uncreated Light

A 6th century design found in the Hagia Sophia
Constantinople/Istanbul

"I am the sun that rises each moment like a new day."
— Jesus, speaking to Saint Symeon, in a vision[241]

We call attention here to a late Medieval Byzantine saint, Symeon the New Theologian (d. 1022), who is of particular interest as a precursor to what has become known as hesychast tradition within Christian Orthodoxy.[242] He is of relevance to the topics of the divine light, the cosmic and interior fire, the situation of repentance (and associated tears) within the overall schema of Christian spiritual formation, and relations with one's elder or spiritual guide. As a matter of terminology, we have used the expression "divine light" above.

More often, in connection with St. Symeon, there is reference to the "uncreated light." In Symeon's visionary experience, the image of the rising sun is also the descent of the divine sun upon him and within him. It is this descent that enables him to ascend in spirit. For our purposes in this present text, "divine light," "uncreated light" and the divine Presence associated with descent into the vicinity of the heart are all equivalent notions. Centuries earlier than Symeon, St. John Chrysostom had said, "Find the door of your heart, you will discover it is the door of the kingdom of God."[243] The tradition of illumination goes at least as far back as Plato's Parable of the Cave, within the

---

[241] As quoted in Thomas Matus, *Yoga and the Jesus Prayer*, previously cited, p. 65. See Matus for further sourcing in *Catéchèses* [Catechetical Sermons or Discourses], edited by Basile Krivochéine.

[242] Two of the more useful and accessible works concerned with Symeon the New Theologian, for readers with a general interest in the various contexts, are Hannah Hunt, *A Guide to St. Symeon the New Theologian*, previously cited, and Thomas Matus, *Yoga and the Jesus Prayer*, previously cited.

[243] As quoted in Anthony Bloom, *Beginning to Pray* (Mahwah, New Jersey: Paulist Press, 1970), p. 46.

Hellenic stream, and into Merkabah (or Chariot) mysticism within the Judaic stream.[244] Within Christian tradition, many of the hesychast themes can be found in (Proto-Hesychast) thinkers and writers between the time of Saint Basil the Great (d. 379) and the time of Saint Symeon the New Theologian in the tenth and eleventh centuries. These themes include "monasticism, dark and light mysticism, an emphasis on the heart, *theōsis*, the humanity of Christ, *penthos*, and unceasing prayer."[245]

Within Sufi thought, Al-Ghazali (d. 1111) considered that light is "that which reveals" or that which leads to an awareness of transcendence.[246] This is an important insight to bear in mind throughout this present text. The tradition reached its zenith within Byzantine hesychast tradition in which there can be participation in the uncreated light. Humankind can, in this way, enter into the life or world (the glory) of the Holy Trinity.[247] Hesychast participation in the uncreated *light* is just one aspect of a broader topic of energetics. With Saint Gregory Palamas (d. 1357 or 1359), there is concern with the uncreated *energies* of God.[248]

---

[244] In reference to the Western philosophical tradition as commonly taught in the wake of the Enlightenment, Peter Kingsley has referred to the existence of a "tradition behind the tradition" that Nicholas Laos has also referred to as "illuminist" tradition. This tradition also appears in Islamicate cultures with the school of Suhrawardi. Certain continuities exist between the school of Suhrawardi and the Pre-Socratics.

[245] From the Abstract of Theodore Sabo, "The Proto-Hesychasts: Origins of mysticism in the Eastern church," 2012, Ph.D. dissertation in Theology, North-West University (Potchefstroom Campus), South Africa. On-line at: <https://dspace.nwu.ac.za/bitstream/handle/10394/8218/Sabo_T.pdf> (Accessed 11/7/2020)

[246] See Zora Hesova, "The Notion of Illumination in the Perspective of Ghazali's Mishkat al-Anwar," *Journal of Islamic Thought and Civilization*, Volume 2, Issue 2, Fall 2012, pp. 65-85, pp. 72, 80. On-line at: <https://journals.umt.edu.pk/index.php/JITC/article/view/334> (Accessed 8/13/2020)

[247] With regard to the roots of this illuminist tradition, see Nicolas Laos, *The Hesychastic Illuminism and the Theory of the Third Light* (London: White Crane Publishing, 2014).

[248] Concern with the divine "energies" is much older than Christian hesychasm. These energies are central to Kashmir Shaivism where they associate, within Shaivist myth, with the figure of Kali, the Shakti or consort of Shiva. Concern with these energies is a feature of Tantrism in general,

Another way to appreciate Symeon is to recall the work of Owen Barfield in which he writes about "original participation," the ancient condition of the human race prior to the emergence of what we might call individuals from out of the collective (group) experience. What we know of St. Symeon shows him to be a contributor to the on-going process, in his time, of individuation. We say this based on the valuation that Symeon gives to personal experience of the Spirit as authenticating one's spiritual authority, as opposed to reliance on external authority. Stelios Ramfos writes:

> His idea about a conscious sense of the divine light, that is, of an unmediated reception of the Holy Spirit, was so provocative that it brought him into conflict with the ecclesiastical establishment, a confrontation that cost Symeon dearly. It was provocative at the time, but today it proves exceptionally interesting, because it gives us the measure of *the individuality that was then making a cautious appearance* in Byzantine society and touched on the realm of theology.[249]

We made reference above, in Section 3, "The Imaginarium (Oratory)," to the divine light or the Glory and to the indistinguishability of inner and outer perception in this instance. Andrew Louth (Emeritus Professor of Patristic and Byzantine Studies, Durham University) writes about this as follows:

> This experience, if it is genuine and not a hallucination, is a sign that the intellect has attained the state that Evagrios calls *apatheia*, a state of transcendence over disturbing thoughts and feelings: "This is a proof of *apatheia*, when the intellect begins

whether Shaivist or Buddhist. For discussion of the analog of Buddhist Tantra, see Christopher Emory-Moore, "Clear and Uncreated: The Experience of Inner Light in Gelug-pa Tantrism and Byzantine Hesychasm," *Buddhist-Christian Studies*, Volume 36, 2016, pp. 117-131.

[249] Stelios Ramfos, "Inconceivable Nothingness: The Philokalia and the roots of modern Greek Nihilism: An essay in philosophical anthropology," an English translation, p. 226. Emphasis added. On-line at: <https://www.academia.edu/24236505/Inconceivable_Nothingness> (Accessed 6/23/2020)

to see its own light, and remains calm during the visions of sleep, and can look at things with serenity."[250]

Maximos Lavriotis (Peterhouse, Cambridge) writes this:

Another Eastern father, St. Symeon the New Theologian, suggested that once it becomes impossible for any humans to any longer be deified, then the end of the world shall come—simply because there would no longer be any purpose for the universe to exist. So, we are still here because we are ascending (some human beings are still ascending) to God, and thereby responding to the descending act of His Incarnation. The primeval purpose of the creation (i.e. God's union with us through His Incarnation) has already been realized. Because nothing can stop God from claiming His own "baggage" in its entirety, there is also the tremendous reassurance that Christ is to inevitably realize also our union with Him and, by all means, be united with all. This dynamic idea explains why nobody is to be lost, in the sense that nobody is to remain unjustly possessed by any adversary or evil power. This is the most powerful and convincing interpretation of St. Paul's expression that "God will be all, in all," (I Corinthians 15:28) in the sense that God will have a way to be united even with those who do not deserve this ineffable union, tremendous though their suffering may be because of the union. St. Maximus has put it this way: "He will make everything—the whole of humanity—His own out of His ineffable goodness. Nobody is to be lost, since, having identified Himself with humanity as a whole, He will claim the whole of humanity as His own Self, as everything which has been created by Him really and eternally belongs to Him."[251]

---

[250] Andrew Louth, "Light, vision and religious experience in Byzantium," in Matthew T. Kapstein, editor, *The Presence of Light: Divine Radiance and Religious Experience*. (Chicago: University of Chicago Press, 2004), pp. 85-103, pp. 86-87.

[251] Maximos Lavriotis, "St. Maximus' cosmology and modern astrophysics," September 19, 1998. On-line at: <https://digilander.libero.it/gogmagog1/ortodossia/Cosmology.htm> (Accessed 6/14/2020)

Alexander Kalomiros wrote as follows about Saint Symeon:

> Saint Symeon the New Theologian says that it is not what man does which counts in eternal life but what he is, whether he is like Jesus Christ our Lord, or whether he is different and unlike Him. He says, "In the future life the Christian is not examined if he has renounced the whole world for Christ's love, or if he has distributed his riches to the poor or if he fasted or kept vigil or prayed, or if he wept and lamented for his sins, or if he has done any other good in this life, but he is examined attentively if he has any similitude with Christ, as a son does with his father."
> — From Kalomiros, "The River of Fire"

> "Do not deceive yourself," says Saint Symeon the New Theologian, "God is fire and when He came into the world, and became man, He sent fire on the earth, as He Himself says; this fire turns about searching to find material—that is a disposition and an intention that is good—to fall into and to kindle; and for those in whom this fire will ignite, it becomes a great flame, which reaches Heaven.... This flame at first purifies us from the pollution of passions and then it becomes in us food and drink and light and joy, and renders us light ourselves because we participate in His light" (Discourse 78).
> — From Kalomiros, "The River of Fire"

Within hesychast tradition generally, there is emphasis on *penthos* or repentance as an essential pre-condition to fuller participation in the divine or uncreated light. The cleansing (of the eye of the heart) occurs of itself when one allows oneself to become still, to enter into the stillness.[252] What we are chiefly cleansed from are "the passions,"

---

[252] Within a certain stream of hesychast tradition, the "gift of tears" that effects this cleansing can be considered a kind of initiation into this tradition. Hannah Hunt points out that, for Symeon, the tears shed at birth are expressive of the tears of this life present here in earth and the fact that a baby cries as soon as it is born is proof that mourning is an essential part of the human condition. For Symeon, tears shed in adult life, however, are more heavenly; the presence of the Holy Spirit in penitent tears indicates new birth

which—by definition—are anything but still. To enter into the stillness is to experience the falling away of the passions. The passions seem to arise in some proportion to the extent of our divided condition. Thomas Matus writes:

> ... in the concrete order of things, the human being is, as Symeon says, a "double being," a composition of opposites and a living contradiction. The other polarities in the world are rendered more acute and irreconcilable by the divisions within our own being. Through the incarnation of God in Jesus Christ, these divisions are ultimately reconciled. Symeon calls him the "double God," who constitutes the unity of microcosm and macrocosm and above all the unity of God and creation.[253]

Perhaps the most important thing we can say about the uncreated light in the hesychast tradition of Saint Symeon is that it is an illumination that (metaphysically) transcends the inner/outer binary or distinction. But having noted that, the illumination is a "seeing from." It is a brightness "within" that illumines—or sees the luminescence in all things. The ontological character of the uncreated light is apparent in the holy icons, where it has been observed that the saints are themselves luminous sources of light. They do not cast shadows.[254]

> God is fire: and He came to send fire on the earth (Luke 12:49) ... If [this fire] is lit in someone, it grows in him until it becomes a great flame and reaches heaven ... The burning of the soul that is inflamed by it does not occur in an unconscious manner ... , but in full assurance and knowledge ... Having entirely purified us from stain of passions, [this fire] becomes our food and drink, illumination and joy within us, and it makes us light by participation ... When the soul ... is united with the divine

---

from above, which turns humans into sons and daughters of God. (Hunt, previously cited, p. 95)

[253] Matus, *op. cit.*, p. 100.

[254] It has been noted above, at page 39, that Jesus Christ himself, in the Gospel accounts, has no apparent "shadow side." His actions on all occasions seem deliberate and not simply reactive.

and immaterial fire ... , *then the body as well becomes by participation the fire of this divine and unspeakable light.*[255]

This illuminist tradition, as we have noted, pre-dates Symeon. Within Christian context, it is rooted in the writings of the Coptic and East Syrian poet theologians.[256] Within this context, Christ himself is the embodiment and exemplar of the light that is both divine and deifying. Concerning this tradition, Professor Tănase writes: "But Christ Himself is deifying light. This light is 'theurgic' in the sense of 'divinising'."[257] George C. Papademetriou (Hellenic College/Holy Cross) writes:

> The "light" is a universal symbol of God and God's Reign, in contrast to darkness and its misery. The symbol of God as "light" was commonly used in Greek philosophy and religious tradition in the mystery religions ("enlightenment": as vision of god or goddess); this was also true in Gnosticism, in the heretical sects of Judaism and Christianity. In the Christian creed Jesus Christ is the Son of God, viewed as "Light of Light," and the entire Christian theology, ethics, and liturgics are imbued by this symbolism of "light." It is true that some Eastern writers speak of God in apophatic terms and symbolism. This is true only in a few neoplatonic theologians who speak of God in an absolute apophatic way. For them, God is beyond, as described in the writings of Dionysius the Areopagite, Maximus the Confessor, and others. However, accor-

---

[255] Jean Darrouzès, editor, [Theological and Ethical Discourses] *Traités théologiques et éthiques*, VII, 1.509-537, as quoted in Metropolitan Hilarion of Volokolamsk, "St. Symeon the New Theologian and his Teaching on the Vision of the Divine Light," *European Journal for Philosophy of Religion*, Summer 2015, Volume 7, Number 2, pp. 3-20, p. 16. Emphasis added.

[256] Among others associated in some way with this tradition, we may note Evagrios, Macarius, Maximos, Symeon the New Theologian, Theophanes of Nicaea, Palamas, Seraphim of Sarov, and Silouan of Athos.

[257] Nichifor Tănase, "Becoming *'all light, all face, all eye'*: Central Aspects of Macarius' Theology," *International Journal of Orthodox Theology*, 2018, Volume 9, Issue 4, pp. 32-116, pp. 32-33. On-line at: <https://www.orthodox-theology.com/media/PDF/4.2018/NichiforTanase.pdf> (Accessed 10/28/2020). In this paper Tănase provides information on the tradition of participation of the body in the uncreated light.

ding to the claim of the apophatic way, "God is light" more than darkness.[258]

The uncreated light is also angelophanic light. Author and poet, Peter O'Leary (School of the Art Institute of Chicago and the University of Chicago) writes:

> The dynamic, intermediary zone between the visible and the invisible is a place of intense focus for the imagination of the visionary poet. Light is quarried and collected from this realm, changed to pure energy in paradise; turned into metaphorical gold in the lower world we inhabit. In the intermediary, visionary realm, every thought is a person, every person is accompanied by an angel. Thinking is angelomorphosis. Enlightenment is angelophany.[259]

Visionary connection with this "dynamic, intermediary zone" is the critical factor in our ability to recognize and to shape an arriving future that we would wish to inhabit.

The divine light also figures in the autobiography of the medieval German Dominican friar, Henry Suso (d. 1366), as the all-pervasive "Shining Brightness":

> In the first days of his conversion it happened upon the Feast of St. Agnes, when the Convent had breakfasted at midday, that the Servitor went into the choir. He was alone, and he placed himself in the last stall on the prior's side. And he was in much suffering, for a heavy trouble weighed upon his heart. And being there alone, and devoid of all consolations—no one by his side, no one near him—of a sudden his soul was rapt in his

---

[258] George C. Papademetriou, "The Enlightenment of Zen Buddhism and the Hesychastic Vision of the Divine Light," *Journal of Ecumenical Studies*, Volume 50, Issue 1, Winter 2015, p. 57. On-line at: <https://www.academia.edu/ 37538311/the_enlightenment_of_zen_buddhism_and_the_hesychastic_vision _of_the_divine_light> (Accessed 1/7/2021)

[259] From Peter O'Leary, "An imaginal homage to Joseph Donahue," undated essay at *Jacket 2* website. On-line at: <https://jacket2.org/article/imaginal-homage-joseph-donahue> (Accessed 11/9/2020)

body, or out of his body. Then did he see and hear that which no tongue can express.

That which the Servitor saw had no form neither any manner of being; yet he had of it a joy such as he might have known in the seeing of the shapes and substances of all joyful things. His heart was hungry, yet satisfied, his soul was full of contentment and joy: his prayers and hopes were all fulfilled. And the Friar could do naught but contemplate this Shining Brightness, and he altogether forgot himself and all other things. Was it day or night? He knew not. It was, as it were, a manifestation of the sweetness of Eternal Life in the sensations of silence and of rest. Then he said, "If that which I see and feel be not the Kingdom of Heaven, I know not what it can be: for it is very sure that the endurance of all possible pains were but a poor price to pay for the eternal possession of so great a joy."

This ecstasy lasted from half an hour to an hour, and whether his soul were in the body or out of the body he could not tell. But when he came to his senses it seemed to him that he returned from another world. And so greatly did his body suffer in this short rapture that it seemed to him that none, even in dying, could suffer so greatly in so short a time. The Servitor came to himself moaning, and he fell down upon the ground like a man who swoons. And he cried inwardly, heaving great sighs from the depth of his soul and saying, "Oh, my God, where was I and where am I?" And again, "Oh, my heart's joy, never shall my soul forget this hour!" He walked, but it was but his body that walked, as a machine might do. None knew from his demeanor that which was taking place within. But his soul and his spirit were full of marvels; heavenly lightnings passed and repassed in the deeps of his being, and it seemed to him that he walked on air. And all the powers of his soul were full of these heavenly delights. He was like a vase from which one has taken a precious ointment, but in which the perfume long remains.[260]

---

[260] From *The Life of Henri Suso by Himself* as reproduced in Evelyn Underhill, *Mysticism: A Study in Nature and Development of Spiritual Consciousness* (Grand Rapids, Michigan: Christian Classics Ethereal Library, first published in 1911),

Hundreds of years later than Saint Symeon and Henry Suso, there appears in Russia the purported account of the conversation between the landowner, Nikolay Motovilov (d. 1879), and Saint Seraphim of Sarov (d. 1833). The experience itself could be regarded as an experience of the uncreated light, although that expression does not appear in the conversation. Here is an abbreviated account of this famous and remarkable conversation concerned with acquisition of the Holy Spirit:

Then Father Seraphim took me very firmly by the shoulders and said: "We are both in the Spirit of God now, my son. Why don't you look at me?"

I replied: "I cannot look, Father, because your eyes are flashing like lightning. Your face has become brighter than the sun, and my eyes ache with pain."

Father Seraphim said: "Don't be alarmed, your Godliness! Now you yourself have become as bright as I am. You are now in the fullness of the Spirit of God yourself; otherwise you would not be able to see me as I am."

Then, bending his head towards me, he whispered softly in my ear: "Thank the Lord God for His unutterable mercy to us! You saw that I did not even cross myself; and only in my heart I prayed mentally to the Lord God and said within myself: 'Lord, grant him to see clearly with his bodily eyes that descent of Thy Spirit which Thou grantest to Thy servants when Thou art pleased to appear in the light of Thy magnificent glory.' And you see, my son, the Lord instantly fulfilled the humble prayer of poor Seraphim. How then shall we not thank Him for this unspeakable gift to us both? Even to the greatest hermits, my son, the Lord God does not always show His mercy in this way. This grace of God, like a loving mother, has been pleased to comfort your contrite heart at the intercession of the Mother of God herself. But why, my son, do you not look me in the eyes? Just look, and don't be afraid! The Lord is with us!"

After these words I glanced at his face and there came over me an even greater reverent awe. Imagine in the center of the sun, in the dazzling light of its midday rays, the face of a man

---

p. 173. On-line at: <https://ccel.org/ccel/underhill/mysticism/mysticism> (Accessed 1/25/2021)

talking to you. You see the movement of his lips and the changing expression of his eyes, you hear his voice, you feel someone holding your shoulders; yet you do not see his hands, you do not even see yourself or his figure, but only a blinding light spreading far around for several yards and illumining with its glaring sheen both the snow-blanket which covered the forest glade and the snow-flakes which besprinkled me and the great Elder. You can imagine the state I was in![261]

Whatever the circumstances of its publication, the fact of its widespread circulation is a testament to something thought to be of value in this conversation to a number of Christian people. It may also be worth nothing that, both in the instance of Saint Symeon and in the instance of Saint Seraphim, the uncreated light is experienced in an inter-personal situation.

The tradition of the uncreated light or the illuminist tradition has many dimensions. Another perspective on the tradition comes from Saint Silouan the Athonite (d. 1938). For him, experience of the Uncreated Light is participation in the passionlessness of God:

The passionless person is full of love, pity, concern; but all these proceed from God acting in that person. Passionlessness may be defined as the acquiring of the Holy Spirit; as Christ living in us. Passionlessness is the light of new life inspiring in us new feelings and thoughts, a new light of eternal understanding. The holy Fathers of the Church define passionlessness as the resurrection of the soul before the general resurrection of the dead.[262]

---

[261] Excerpted from "St. Seraphim of Sarov's Conversation with Nicholas Motovilov: A Wonderful Revelation to the World," on-line at: <http://orthodoxinfo.com/praxis/wonderful.aspx> (Accessed 1/3/2021). The publication of this conversation was not, however, without some controversy. See the account posted on-line by John Sanidopoulos at: <https://www.johnsanidopoulos.com/2020/01/the-authenticity-of-conversation.html> (Accessed 1/3/2021)

[262] "Saint Silouan of Mount Athos (1866-1938): A Short Life History," *Sourozh: a journal of Orthodox life and thought*, Issue 20[?], p. 177. As quoted in Stefan Mastilovic, "A Never-Ending Story? The 'Age of the Fathers,' St. Symeon the New Theologian's Notion of Patristic Authority, and the Church Fathers of Modern Times," Bachelor of Theology (Honours) thesis, Sydney

Passionlessness, as described by Saint Silouan, is a consequence of an awareness of the divine Presence. Passionlessness can also be understood to mean a meditative state, whether the body is in stillness or in motion accomplishing an action. As noted further below, states of meditation are also the "place" of reverie.

The range of phenomena signified by the expression, *uncreated light*, is also sometimes referred to as *fotisis*. The sociologist of contemporary Orthodox folk religion, Kyriacos Markides (University of Maine), writes:

> … Fotisis means the vision and the experience of the *Uncreated Light*, God's Divine light. It is considered the most prized gift of the Spirit superseding all other gifts, the real goal of the spiritual struggle. It is the mystical contemplation of God's presence in the world that floods the soul with exquisite joy. It is the experience of Moses on Mt. Sinai, of Jesus on Mt. Tabor, of the Apostles at Pentecost and of all the great saints throughout the ages.[263]

In the same paper, Professor Markides also reproduces the following account from Elder Paisios (d. 1994):

> One night while I was in my cell reciting the *Efche*, the Jesus Prayer," he reported, "I began to feel overwhelmed by a heavenly joy. My dark cell, lit by only one candle, began gradually to fill up with a most beautiful whiteblue light. At first the light was very intense. But then my eyes got accustomed to its brilliance. It was the *Uncreated Light* manifesting Itself! I stayed in that condition for several hours and lost

College of Divinity, St. Andrew's Greek Orthodox Theologian College, 2014, p. 45. On-line at: <https://www.academia.edu/34410511/A_NEVER_ENDING_STORY_The_Age_of_the_Fathers_St_Symeon_the_New_Theol ogian_s_Notion_of_Patristic_Authority_and_the_Church_Fathers_of_Moder n_Times> (Accessed 1/7/2021)

[263] Kyriacos C. Markides, "Eastern Orthodox Mysticism and Transpersonal Theory," *The Journal of Transpersonal Psychology*, Volume 40, Number 2, Fall 2008, pp. 178-198 On-line at: <https://pdfs.semanticscholar.org/9bcb/f3c9735a53a280e420c4465fc1bc680df0d9.pdf> (Accessed 1/21/2021)

every sensation of worldly matters. I lived in a different, spiritual world, much different from this world of carnality.

While in that state I was exposed to heavenly visions and extraordinary experiences. Without noticing, many hours passed by. Then the *Uncreated Light* began to recede and I returned to my previous condition. I was hungry and I ate a piece of dried bread. I was thirsty and drank some water. I was tired and sat down to rest. I felt like an animal and deplored myself for being no different than the beasts. This natural humility was born inside me as a consequence of the change in my situation. From the spiritual condition I was in, I had entered into this one and, perceiving the difference, there was little left for me but to condemn and loathe myself. When I walked outside I thought it was still night with a full moon. Not far from me there lived another brother in his hermitage. I walked there and asked him for the time. It was ten in the morning. The *Uncreated Light* was so intense that I thought the light of day was like the night and the Sun was like the Moon![264]

Professor Markides further writes that "The experience of the *Uncreated Light* may also take other more concrete forms. It may bring about dramatic healing phenomena and serve as a shield against external dangers." This is illustrated in the account that Markides provides concerning the Soviet-era imprisonment of Fr. Arseny together with a young prisoner named Alexei. Markides concludes that account:

It is important to note here that the experience of the *Uncreated Light* can unexpectedly befall any human being, regardless of his or her station in life. Alexei was not a believer yet he had the experience of the *Uncreated Light* which not only saved his life but also transformed him as a person. Saul was a persecutor of Christians until he fell off his horse on the road to Damascus and was temporarily blinded by the brilliance of the *Uncreated Light.* That experience catapulted him not only to fulfill his extraordinary historic mission as St. Paul, Apostle of the

---

[264] Ibid.

nations but also to provide to Christians the proper understanding of God as unconditional and total Love.[265]

Experience of the uncreated light is simply another manifestation of divine grace that may unexpectedly flood the thirsty soul when it is parched and dry. Experience of the uncreated light also signifies the possibility of the return or recurrence of another kind of culture—a cardiocentric culture. In another context, the literature and philosophy scholar, Nadezhda Grigoryeva (University of Tübingen), characterizes this type of culture as follows:

> The human body has undergone various refigurations in cultural history. Some thinkers have viewed the mind as the center of human beings. Others, like Freud, considered man to be a phallocentric creature. Plenty of cultures, however, have been centered on the heart rather than the head, or something else in their understanding of human beings. In these cultures the heart has played the main role not only in the human body, but also in human thought. Classical Latin used the heart (*cor*) as a synonym for thought, memory, mind, soul and spirit. The heart's *shen* was a centre of personality in Taoism; the spiritual heart *hridaya* was a receptacle of atman in Hinduism; according to Sufism the *kalb* ("heart") was a paramount human organ that provided people with integrity of cognition. The cardiocentric theory of mind seems to have reached its pinnacle in Buddhism, with the phenomenon of "heart cognition" (*Prajna-paramita*). Moreover, the "intelligent" heart also played the chief role in Hesychasm etc.[266]

In cardiocentric cultures, preeminent value associates with the heart. Value attaches to effort to connect or relate all things to the heart. Ancient Egypt was a culture of this type. Recognition, revival and re-

---

[265] Ibid.

[266] Nadezhda Grigoryeva, "Speak Heart…: Vladimir Sorokin's Mystical Language," in Tine Roesen & Dirk Uffelmann, editors, *Vladimir Sorokin's Languages*, Volume 11 in the *Slavica Bergensia* series, University of Bergen, 2013. On-line at: <https://boap.uib.no/books/sb/catalog/view/9/8/163-1> (Accessed 2/25/2021)

animation of cardiocentric cultures in our time are essential to subversion of the slavery that is called "Babylon."[267]

10. Leaving Babylon

Chaldean/Babylonian sculpture

Babylon is enthralldom to all that is mechanical—the hidden and not-so-hidden engine of slavery.[268] It is the engine not only of slavery in an explicit and obvious sense, but also of colonialism and systemic racism, all of which are dimensions of the Babylon system. Emblematic of this enthralldom to the mechanical that is characteristic of Babylon are the national programs of space exploration that are expressions of the collective ego in search of conquest. Reverie, as it has been discussed in this book, can be understood as humankind's hidden doorway out of ideologies of every kind—the way out of Babylon and its slavery to the

---

[267] In Byzantine culture, the prevalence of the class of objects known as *enkolpia*—crosses, medallions adorned with Christian imagery, and miniature reliquaries, among others, worn around the neck—served as a powerful means of forming the heart-focused subjectivity of Byzantine selves. See Ivan Drpić, "The Enkolpion: Object, Agency, Self," in *Gesta*, Volume 57, Number 2, Fall 2018. On-line at: <https://doi.org/10.1086/698842> (Accessed 2/25/2021). This heart-focused subjectivity provides the surest orientation of reverie, with which we are concerned in this book, towards that which is life-giving.

[268] Among some scholars, the Babylon system is referred to as "dominator culture," an expression that refers to a model of society where fear and force maintain rigid understandings of power and superiority within a hierarchical structure. Riane Eisler popularized this term in her book, *The Chalice and the Blade: Our History, Our Future* (HarperCollins, 1987). Other theorists, including Terence McKenna and bell hooks, have expanded on the implications and impact of dominator culture. What we mean by "Babylon" in the context of this book is not merely all that is mechanical, but that which seeks domination through (or by means of) the mechanical. In support of multi-cultural environments, however, I believe it is possible to speak of "prevailing" cultures without implying "domination"—because all cultures potentially have some gift to offer the planet.

mechanical. To perceive the world as the Babylon we are leaving behind it is necessary to know one thing: We came from Paradise and we are journeying to Paradise.[269] But Paradise is not simply origin and destination in time. As a present reality it is also a perception and, in the words of Douglas Christie (Loyola Marymount University), a practice.[270] On the way, we may pass through many heavens and many hells. Consider the tragedy of families that have never learned to sing. We are leaving that circumstance behind. Saints are not heroes, although some may be. Saints *see* differently—their perception is different. Their perception is illuminated by the divine light that penetrates the darkness. Contemporary Russian poet and translator, Olga Sedakova, writes as follows about what it is that a saint sees:

> Some years ago I happened to be at the service in a distant village church. It was the day of commemoration of "All the Saints Who Shone Forth in the Russian Land," as our official Church calendar calls the second Sunday after the Pentecost. At the end of the service, as the rule prescribes, the priest said his homily. The priest was in his sixties and looked rather tired and not too healthy (later I was told that he came to Tula region from Chernobyl). He said: "As a rule, people adore a Saint only after his or her death. Yes, when they are dead and glorified, we love them so much: they are our Saints! We are proud to be their compatriots, to be born in the same land, or city, or village. We even expect them to protect us much warmer and with better care than they do the others, because we are their neighbors and almost their relatives. But in their lifetime Saints, normally, are not held in respect, they do not enjoy either support or sympathy on behalf of their neighbors. Just the opposite: people are disposed to scorn and laugh at such persons. People, as a rule, find them miserable and

---

[269] As the scholar of mysticism, Andrew Harvey, has remarked, "The ultimate nature of reality is bliss." From the video conversation between Andrew Harvey and Scott Catamas, June 2020, at 26:35. On-line at: <https://youtu.be/DAAX4glqXaQ> (Accessed 7/20/2020)

[270] Douglas E. Christie, "Practicing Paradise: Contemplative Awareness and Ecological Renewal," *Anglican Theological Review*, Volume 94, Number 2, 2012, pp. 281-303. On-line at: <https://digitalcommons.lmu.edu/theo_fac/109/> (Accessed 8/14/2020)

foolish, and the mode of their life—absurd: it's unheard of, nobody behaves like that! But the chief thing in all of this is that everybody is sure that a Saint (their future Saint) looks at everything in a wrong, fantastic, stupid way. In people's mind, a living Saint can't appreciate the real state of things in 'our world' which they pretend to know perfectly; he (or she) proves to be less experienced, than a child. And his (or her) fatal blindness is sad, ridiculous and irritating. But, my dear friends," the priest went on, and his tone suddenly changed and now it was almost triumphant, "there are just Saints who see everything in the right, realistic and practical way. They, and nobody else, do see our world as it is. And what do they see? They see our Earth—and all our world—flying towards the Lord. Flying, like a bird, staring at one point, her wings out-stretched like that (he tried to mimic the flight) to the dear final Meeting."[271]

To see our Earth and all our world flying toward the Lord is a directed mode of reverie in the imaginal. The imaginal overlays everything and is the sophianic channel of divine energies—ascending and descen-ding—between Heaven and Earth. And what is it that the saints and the people[272] (*sobornost*) are flying from? They are flying away from Babylon and its many modes of enslavement! *Sobornost* or the organic togetherness of spiritual community is the state or condition from which Babylon has fallen.

We are the little dog whose name is faithfulness and hunger.[273] The little dog who waits impatiently but confidently for crumbs from its master's table may bring to mind these words from St. Basil the Great: "Because we did not fast, we were chased out of Paradise; let us fast

---

[271] From the first section of Olga Sedakova's essay, "The Light of Life: Some Remarks on the Russian Orthodox Perception," July/August 2005, at her website. On-line at: <http://www.olgasedakova.com/eng/Moralia/270> (Accessed 11/13/2020)

[272] The "Christ people," in the terminology of Rudolf Steiner.

[273] Recall the performance by Coleman Barks of Rumi's poem, "Love Dogs." As Rumi said, "Give your life to be one of them." On-line at: <https://youtu.be/UF4_KZfIfVI> (Accessed 8/28/2020)

now, so that someday we return there."[274] The little dog may also stand in for the entire animal realm that is enduring such suffering. We claim for ourselves the Golden Chain of saints[275] but, like the bodhisattvas, we will not forget the creatures living in shadow, including the animals dependent upon God alone for their daily bread.[276] The paradise to which we are journeying is the Eternal Now permeated with the fragrance of the divine Presence—the Eternal Now that comprehends both past and future unfoldings.[277] This is what is being sought in every reverie. Paradise is the reveriesial function of the *silsila* in Sufism

----

[274] A common translation from Sermon 1 on fasting from homilies for Lent by St. Basil the Great in J. P. Migne's *Patrologia graeca*. The Greek and another English translation can be found on-line at: <https://bible.org/seriespage/appendix-1-basil%e2%80%99s-sermons-about-fasting> (Accessed 10/9/2020)

[275] In Christian spiritual (or monastic) culture, the Golden Chain is understood to mean that each successive spiritual father or mother is a link connecting him or her back in time to the apostles and to Jesus himself. See Hannah Hunt, previously cited, p. 43. Hagiography and the lives of saints can be understood as both object and fruit of reverie as discussed in this present book.

[276] Vegetarian diet is fundamental to spiritual practice. See the short videos by Fordham University ethicist, Charles Camosy, on-line at: <https://www.charlescamosy.com/ask-charlie-anything> (Accessed 7/20/2020). Among the books on the subject, a recent one of particular note is Katherine Wills Perlo, *Kinship and Killing: The Animal in World Religions* (New York: Columbia University Press, 2009). Reflect on the lives the saints who are known to have particular association or care for animals. These include St. Mammas, St. Tryphon, St. Iakovos of Evia, St. Vlasios (Blaise) the Hieromartyr of Sebaste, St. Modestos (Bishop of Jerusalem), and St. Melangell the Righteous of Wales. See the *Full of Grace and Truth* blog entries at: <http://full-of-grace-and-truth.blogspot.com/search/label/Animals> (Accessed 8/15/2020)

[277] Saint Maximus the Confessor, in his *Ambiguum* 41, outlines five cosmic divisions which it was man's original purpose to unite: the division of the uncreated from the created; the division of the intelligible world from the sensible world; the division of heaven from earth; the division of paradise from the inhabited world; and the division of male from female. Paradise can be defined as the unification, through Christ, of these primordial divisions. For an English translation of Maximus, see Andrew Louth, *Maximus the Confessor* (New York: Routledge, 1996).

or of the Golden Chain of saints more generally.[278] There is a sense in which we may think of reverie *as* Paradise and Paradise *as* reverie.

We are leaving Babylon—or is it, rather, that we are learning to *inhabit* Babylon—learning to sing in a strange land? If we are learning to inhabit Babylon, it is as the three young men in the fiery furnace who were not consumed by the flames.[279] This image—of the three young men in the fiery furnace—is the image of initiatory experience. If the rite of baptism is no longer the initiatory experience it once was in the early Church, then a need for our time is for initiatory groups that do recognize and honor the dual origin of humankind—an origin both in heaven and in Earth.[280] Gurdjieff had an ambivalent feeling about the church of his day.[281] Perhaps he felt the Church itself, while having a dual nature (as does the human person) with roots in both Heaven and Earth, has allowed itself to forget its amphibious nature.

In the cosmogony of the German Christian mystic and philosopher, Jacob Boehme, there may be some question of the metaphysical "place" of the nothingness of the *ungrund* as it relates to God or to what is sometimes called the godhead. Formulated as a question: "Is the chaotic nothingness within God or is it over against God and

---

[278] There is a sense in which we choose our ancestors or the saints to whom we adhere in the journey to Paradise. The Ethiopian Christian national epic, *Kebra Nagast*, can be regarded as an example of this.

[279] This is a reference to the story of Shadrach, Meshach, and Abednego in Chapter 3 of the Old Testament Book of Daniel. These are three Hebrew men thrown into a fiery furnace by Nebuchadnezzar, king of Babylon, when they refuse to bow down to the king's image. The three are preserved from harm and the king sees four men walking in the flames, "the fourth ... like a son of God."

[280] An example of one such recently formed group is the Communion of the Mystic Rose: "An initiatory fellowship of spiritual pilgrims in passionate pursuit of the inner flowering of Wisdom; a canonical, vowed religious community of the Episcopal Church, with deep roots in esoteric Christianity and the ancient Western Mysteries. The heart of our charism is the authentic reclamation of Catholic Christianity as an initiatory Mystery Tradition." From their website at: <https://www.mysticrose.org/> (Accessed 9/14/2020)

[281] According to Joseph Azize, scholar and author of an important study of Gurdjieff published by Oxford University Press in 2020. That study is titled *Gurdjieff: Mysticism, Contemplation, and Exercises.* Joseph Azize is also a priest in the Maronite Catholic Church, working chiefly in the Chancery, and is an honorary associate at the University of Sydney (Australia).

other than God?" The Latin phrase, *extra Ecclesiam nulla salus*, which means, in English, "outside the Church there is no salvation," can be read in a way that is similarly ambiguous. The chaotic nothingness that is the world both is and is not comprehended by the Church as organically all-comprehensive divine reality. The divine wisdom participates in this ambiguity. By analogy, the unconscious is both a personal unconscious and a collective unconscious on varying scales. Whatever wisdom one may acquire in a personal lifetime, it includes attention to the unconscious as source of both help on our journey and hindrance or resistance.

<u>Wisdom schools.</u> In times of duress in particular regions of planet Earth, wisdom school begin to form. It is probably more accurate to say that wisdom schools begin to become more *visible*, from within the general public, to persons searching for guidance. Among the various true things that can be said about wisdom schools is that they are concerned with a certain kind of alchemy, which is to say they are concerned with the art and science of transformations.

In alchemical lore there is a saying—perform no operation until all has become water. (Petrus Bonus of Ferrara, a late medieval alchemist, had said: "*Solutio* is the root of alchemy.") Among the many possible meanings of this is the understanding of a symbolic association of water with the emotional life. Actions are best taken when the passions are dissipated—when the waters are still and the mirror of one's awareness is clear. When the mirror is clear (the "waters are still"), one *sees* more, *hears* more, *remembers* more—*understands* more than one otherwise would.

When the waters are still, transformations can occur. A concise name for this stillness of the waters is *meditation*. Within every authentic wisdom school, whatever its root spiritual tradition, meditation has a central place. It can be noted here that states of meditation are, par excellence, the "place" of reverie. Reverie, as suggested in various ways throughout this present book, is a dynamism that takes us somewhere—that even enables us to become what we are not yet, but what we are meant to be. How does it do this? By allowing us to "see" (to envision) what we, in truth, already are. This is a kind of recognition that occurs—a recognition (a seeing or envisioning) of the human *telos*. In his *Psychology and Alchemy*, Carl Jung wrote of alchemy in this way:

It always remains an obscure point whether the ultimate transformations in the alchemical process ought to be sought more in the material or more in the spiritual realm. Actually, however, the question is wrongly put: there was no "either-or" for that age, but there did exist an intermediate realm between mind and matter, i.e., a psychic realm of subtle bodies whose characteristic it is to manifest themselves in mental as well as material form. This is the only view that makes sense of alchemical ways of thought, which must otherwise appear non-sensical.[282]

Psychotherapist, Robert Romanyshyn (Pacifica Graduate Institute), writes of the psychoidal archetype in Jung by which he means to point out a complementarity of realms (such as conscious and unconscious) to which the "either-or" binary does not apply (as if, for example, in the language of quantum physics, wave and particle are thought of as simultaneous reality). In the quote above, however, we want to avoid identifying, as Jung seems to do, the "spiritual" with the "mental." Given that caveat, this is a good description of the working of the imaginal—of the presence of the imaginal within the everyday world. The imaginal, however, ought not be understood as simply an "inner" human phenomenon, as if it were a product of the human psyche. The imaginal is not simply either "inner" or "outer." The Cartesian binary does not apply. Reverie, as a manifestation of the imaginal, takes us somewhere, but this somewhere both is and is not here in this place where we now are. This is also the nature of the Kingdom of Heaven. The saints live and move and have their being in the Kingdome of Heaven, which both is and is not the everyday world that we inhabit. To use the language of Gurdjieff, their "centers of gravity" have shifted from World 48 to World 24.

We are discussing wisdom schools in this section on Leaving Babylon. A reason why we are considering wisdom school at this

---

[282] Carl Jung, *Psychology and Alchemy*, Volume 12 in the *Collected Works of C. G. Jung*, Bollingen Series (Princeton, New Jersey: Princeton University Press, 1968, 1980), paragraph 394, as quoted in Robert D. Romanyshyn, "The Metaphor or Alchemy and the Alchemy of Metaphor: Working in the Space between Presence and Absence," April 24, 2009, on-line at: <http://www.robertromanyshyn.com/files/documents/The-Metaphor-of-Alchemy-and-the-Alchemy-of-Metaphor.pdf> (Accessed 12/13/2020)

juncture in this present text is because there is a paradox about Babylon and also about Egypt. Although both Babylon and Egypt were experienced as oppressive and enslaving, these cultures were also recognized as having preserved a perennial wisdom.

The goal of Christian wisdom school is to enable the possibility of marrying together the two natures or two worlds—the worlds of heaven and of Earth—within ourselves and within the cultures we generate and inhabit.[283] What this means in practice is that Kingdom of Heaven is seen to be grounding itself in Earth. Jesus Christ is regarded as emblematic or exemplar of this marrying together of the two natures.[284] Wisdom school highlights the ways in which the Christian faith, in its public manifestations in dogma, doctrine, Eucharist, and iconographic and liturgical arts, functions as a "mystery religion," understood in a certain way.[285] The sacraments are traditionally referred to as mysteries. These and other "mysteries" of the faith are a kind of showing, an unveiling, for those who are prepared to see, to hear, and to feel.[286] In the words of Wayne Kraus (publisher, Jacob

---

[283] Reference is made elsewhere in this present text to the dual origins of humankind. An important resource is the Yale Forum on Religion and Ecology, currently directed by Mary Evelyn Tucker & John Grim. On-line at: <https://fore.yale.edu/> (Accessed 1/24/2021)

[284] In the particular instance of Jesus Christ, the Chalcedonian Creed uses the language, "truly God and truly Man," in its definition.

[285] The Christian *sage* serves as hermeneut of the Christian mysteries. This is the content or meaning of Christian hermeticism as activity and not simply collections of propositions. In the church, throughout its history, the sage has played an important role in Christian formation or *paideia*, especially in helping persons to appreciate the riches of the faith, beyond what can be communicated in a limited time within the established catechetical schools. The anonymously authored book, *Meditations on the Tarot: A Journey into Christian Hermeticism*, by Valentin Tomberg, previously cited, is an instance of Christian Hermeticism in literary or written form. There are a number of texts, such as this, that have great value for small group discussion and reflection. Jacob Needleman's *Lost Christianity: A Journey of Rediscovery* (reprint edition, 2003) is another excellent example. It was Jean Gebser's view (in *The Ever-Present Origin*, p. 17) that with the attention to perspective in the Renaissance "[t]he heptagonal cosmos of the ancients and its mystery religions are left behind …."

[286] This is an *embodied* wisdom that is being commended—a wisdom that looks to root persons and communities into the good Earth. Any Christian wisdom school would be well-served to include study of the Catholic social activist,

Boehme Online), "Wisdom teaching is not a body of doctrine that one agrees or disagrees with; it is the light of heaven streaming through an open door."   In our time and in all times, wisdom is not the preserve of any single religious or spiritual tradition.   It is a common human heritage manifested in diverse cultural environments and contexts. Within Abrahamic religious cultures, certain kinds of Sufism may be understood as reflecting and embodying the primordial wisdom of Melchizidek.[287]

For those who would serve wisdom in our time the challenge, however, is to do so in ways that avoid commercialism. Wisdom is not just another consumer product placed into the markets. Babylon in its capitalist deployment, however, is designed to co-opt the efforts of even the most altruistic and well-intentioned. Who are those who would serve wisdom in Christian language?   Saint Symeon wrote: "Listen to what Christ calls out at all times: 'Out of the belly of those who believe in Me there will flow rivers from the divine fountain, water of eternal life.'"[288]   One further note about wisdom is that it arrives from the future that is drawing us forward, not from the past we are leaving behind. Those who serve wisdom look for its glimmerings in the age that is to come.

Peter Maurin, previously mentioned, in its curriculum. Maurin's work is a significant resource for those concerned with understanding both the Babylon system and the means of liberation from it. Important works by Joe Holland and others in the ecological wisdom tradition of Catholic social teaching are published by Pacem in Terris Press <http://www.paceminterrispress.com/>. For a valuable recent study of Anglo-Catholic social teaching in Britain see Philip Turner, *Christian Socialism: The Promise of an Almost Forgotten Tradition* (Eugene, Oregon: Cascade Books / Wipf and Stock Publishers, 2021).

[287] The figure of Melchizedek often associates with the figure of the previously mentioned al-Khidr, the Green One and patron of those who go directly to God without intermediaries. The meeting of Melchizedek and Abraham is also similar in some respects to the meeting of Shams of Tabriz and Rumi. It is said to have been the view of Murat Yagan that both Melchizedek and Shams were messengers from the Source, doing nothing of themselves but carrying enlightenment to someone who could receive it.

[288] From Saint Symeon the New Theologian, *Hymns Of Divine Love*, translated by Fr. George A. Maloney (Denville, New Jersey: Dimension Books, 1975), Hymn 17, p. 71.

<u>A new Eden.</u> Whether we call it the arriving *Age of Mary*, *Age of the Holy Spirit*, the *New Epoch*, or the *New Age*, our search under whatever guise is for one thing only—a new Eden that, we may discover, is always already here.[289] Another metaphor that has roots in the language of scripture is the bridal chamber as the "place" of nondual realization. However, arrival at this place out of time is not the end of our journey. We then become servant of the cosmos or cosmic servant. Recalling the work of Robert Sardello, we will have then begun to see the world as temples of presence. Seen and understood in this way, presence acquires a certain normativity in the governance of what may be called perspectival knowing. Robert Lax, a college classmate and friend of Thomas Merton, was also poet and sage who lived an essentially eremitic or hermit life on the Greek island of Patmos until very late in his life. Lax spoke these words of advice for living in the present circumstances of our time:

> Well, for the record, and I can't say it enough, try to live as purely and as simply and as gently as you can. Relax. Be flexible. Be forgiving. Be creative. Be loving. You are a peacemaker. Those who cross your path may need you, as you may need them. Remember all things under heaven have their special relationship with God. Listen, be discerning, use all the radar you can generate in your waking moments and in your dreams, but don't judge—let God do that. Just try to keep the balance, because you're in it for the long run. We all are.[290]

Early in the twentieth century the Russian philosopher and essayist, Nicholas Berdyaev (d. 1948) had recognized that we are moving into a new phase of world history and wrote about it as follows:

---

[289] These terms are not conceptually identical to the geologic term, *ecozoic*, referenced elsewhere in this present text, but there are overlaps in the range of meanings. The primary distinction has to do with whether the manifestation, in its initiative, is an arising "from below" or a descent "from above." From an understanding of the dual origins of humankind, referenced elsewhere in this present text, both "arising" and "descending" initiatives may converge in service to a common anthropocosmic purpose.

[290] As spoken by Robert Lax to Steve Georgiou and quoted in Steve Theodore Georgiou, *The Way of the Dreamcatcher: Spirit Lessons with Robert Lax: Poet, Peacemaker, Sage* (Ottawa, Canada: Novalis, 2002), p. 247-248.

We are entering upon a period of new spirituality, which will be the counterpart of the present materialism of our world. There will also be a new form of mysticism corresponding to this new period in Christian history. It will henceforth be impossible to oppose the conception of a higher life by pointing to the sinfulness of human nature which must be overcome. There is no longer any room in the world for a merely external form of Christianity based upon custom. It is precisely the mystical and spiritual life which leads to victory over sin. The world is entering upon a new period of catastrophe and crisis when we are being forced to take sides and in which a higher and more intense kind of spiritual life will be demanded from Christians. The sort of Christianity which is purely outward in character and never rises above the level of mediocrity is today on de-cline; while that which possesses eternal significance is growing more intense and stronger.[291]

More recently, John Moriarty coined an expression, "Second Coming Christianity." He wrote: "The Second Coming of Christ which Chris-tians expect and await—it isn't a new or another coming. It is a mys-tical understanding of the First Coming. Second Coming Christianity has been with us, waiting for us, since the beginning."[292]

<u>Living close to the ground (reprised)</u>. What this expression actually means is living in awareness of reality. In our time, a critical factor or element in our present circumstances is the shift that has occurred in what we may call the information landscape. The information com-mons is not being curated. But before we can even begin to consider how this might be done, we need to work on ourselves. One of the goals of this work on ourselves is simplification, choosing to live more simply.

In Section 5 ("Trees and the Green Man") above, we considered some of the symbolic resonances of trees. Learning to live more simply and becoming more aware of our connections with the earth are core elements of what wisdom looks like as we move into the arriving new age, whatever name we may choose to call it. To sit underneath an

---

[291] Nicholas Berdyaev, *Freedom and the Spirit*, translated by Oliver Fielding Clarke (New York: Charles Scribner's Sons, 1935), p. 268.
[292] Moriarty, *Dreamtime*, p. 221.

oak tree at the edge of a forest clearing on a bright warm Summer day,
with no demands on one's time, would be conducive to reverie—
reverie that is also prayer.[293] I imagine that it could also be, in this way,
an ideal setting for the beginnings of wisdom. In such circumstances
we may discover ourselves entering into the dreamtime of the times
and places in which we happen to be. Here is how John Moriarty
described the dreamtime as he reflected upon it in his context of
contemporary Ireland:

> "Altjeringa" is a very beautiful Australian Aboriginal word. To
> me, at any rate, it is very beautiful. It means the Dreamtime, or
> the Dreaming, that was in the beginning. As Aborigines ima-
> gine it, the earth in the beginning was a featureless waste, but
> beings called the Altjeringa Mitjina, the Eternal Ones of the
> Dream, emerged, and they went walkabout, each in his or her
> own way, across this featurelessness; and as they did so, they
> dreamed with the dreaming earth, dreaming now of a river,
> now of a mountain, now of trees; and the rivers, the mountains,
> the trees, the vast variety of things they dreamed of, came to
> exist objectively and independently of the Altjeringa Mitjjina
> who dreamed them. And so it was that the earth as we now
> know it came to be, culture having its origin in things said and
> done in the beginning. [...]
>
> What are poets for in a destitute time? The answer ... is
> that poets must be healers—healers who, healed themselves,
> heal us culturally, heal us, or help to heal us, in the visions and
> myths and rituals by which we live, and to do this effectively
> they must in some sense be Altjeringa Mitjina, temporary ones,
> not eternal ones, of the Dream. [...] The hope is that, however
> ethnically various it might be, there is a European Dreamtime.
> The hope is that Dreamtime always is, is everywhere, is now,
> and that there are people who have access to it. It is sometimes
> the case, isn't it, that individuals are healed as they are at
> present only as a consequence of having been healed as they
> were in their past?

---

[293] Another conducive occasion for reverie would be to sit in the cold winter
before a blazing hearth fire. The importance of both place and occasion for
the imaginal flow that is reverie was noted above, at the end of Section 1 of
this present text.

As with individuals, so, sometimes, with a whole people. Healing in our cultural present will come as a consequence of healing in our cultural past. Out of a healed past a healed present will grow. Out of a re-realized past a re-realized present will emerge. It is as necessary that we realize a past out of which to grow as it is to realize a present and future into which to grow. Our past we have always with us. Our past we must always re-realize. And to do this we need people who can live in our cultural Dreamtime, people who go walkabout, creatively, within the old myths, people who go walkabout into the unknown. It isn't wise, I believe, to do what the originators and executors of the French Revolution did or sought to do. Seized by revolutionary fervor, they would have wiped the slate clean. Intending to hand the last king in the entrails of the last priest, they installed a statue of reason in Notre Dame. But it might be no harm to remember that just as there is an irrational misuse of the irrational, so also there is an irrational misuse of the rational, and that this latter misuse is often as terrible in its consequences as is the former.[294]

If nature herself (the cosmos) is the first revelation, unhurried closeness to nature is also conducive to recollection, to remembrance, to memory of all that the Babylon system attempts to dispel in forgetfulness. It is the remembrance—of who we are, from where we have come, and to where we are journeying—that is the concern of wisdom. This wisdom then begins to engage with the practical, with practice, with the needful work on ourselves, with the question, "How shall we, therefore, live?" Closeness to nature helps us to detach from the hidden and not-so-hidden mechanisms of Babylon. In reverie, our truer selves begin to be shaped, truer selves capable of resisting the temptations of Babylon, because we can envision another way. This other way is life according to the Beatitudes as commended by Jesus in his Sermon on the Mount.[295] How might we understand the forces of

---

[294] Moriarty, *Dreamtime*, pp. vii-viii.

[295] The trilogy of books by Efstratios Papanagiotou, previously cited, provides some of the best written material for facilitating entry into the Christ consciousness that is necessary to enable humans to live in this world according to the Beatitudes. The Taoist text, *Tao Te Ching*, attributed to Lao Tszu (c. 6th – 4th century B.C.) consisting of short chapters of poetry and

resistance within ourselves and within the world at large in this time of transition? Thomas Berry wrote:

> The older tension in human affairs between conservative and liberal based on social orientation is being replaced with the tension between developers and ecologists based on orientation toward the natural world. This new tension is becoming the primary tension in human affairs.
>
> So too the political tension between the empires and the colonies is being replaced by an economic tension between village peoples of the world with their organic modes of agriculture and the transnational corporations with their industrial agriculture.
>
> This new alignment should not be taken as if the ecology movement were a New Left movement or a new liberalism. For the ecology movement has moved the entire basis of the division into a new context. It is no longer a division based on political party or social class or ethnic group. It is a division based on the human as one of the components within the larger community of planet Earth.[296]

<u>Exodus – "under the radar" / the role of music.</u> We have had occasion in this present book to refer to the divine melody. In something like a spiritual psychology, it is this primordial and divine melody that—in the imaginal realms—gently orients us to the six directions, metaphorically speaking. It is our spiritual compass. It is also the "taste" or the "fragrance" that suggests, or indicates, something to us—prior to, or with, the use of words. In the spiritual cosmology of Gurdjieff there are a number of worlds manifesting along what is called the Ray of Creation—worlds that are progressively more dense as they are further from the Absolute or source. In this spiritual cosmology, the more dense the world, the more laws that world is under. Douglas Staley, a

---

philosophical reflection, both profound and paradoxical, proposes a view of life similar to the lily-of-the-field section of the Sermon on the Mount. The John C. H. Wu translation is recommended. See also Thomas Merton's *The Way of Chuang Tzu* (New York: New Directions Publishing, 1997), a book that breathes a similar atmosphere.

[296] Thomas Berry, *The Great Work: Our Way into the Future* (New York: Bell Tower / Crown, reprint edition, 2000), p. 107

long-time student of the Gurdjieff Work, has articulated what he considers to be the important metaphysical and philosophical implications of the Ray of Creation:

- Statements concerning reality are always relative; there is always more to understand.
- Determinism and free will both exist, but in different worlds and at different levels of consciousness.
- No thing is more essential or important than anything else; every thing is of equal value to the Whole.
- The Absolute and the relative can co-exist at the same moment as a higher dimension can interpenetrate a lower dimension, thus acting as the "absolute" for the lower level.
- Everything is connected to everything else; involution and evolution are inextricably intertwined.
- Change is constant in the universe; everything is in motion, entering into existence and dying in a perpetual "dance of life."
- Nothing in the universe is static; everything is in constant movement, either ascending with increasing energy, or descending with decreasing energy.
- All laws in the universe are patterns of ordered relationships; the components of anything always reflect a pattern, but the pattern itself does not exist in the same world as the components.
- Service and the desire to nurture all that exists is the heart of love and the purpose of evolution.[297]

Here is a paradox. While at the same time living in or under the Babylon system, as we begin to cultivate what are called, in the New Testament, "fruits of the Spirit," we experience ourselves as constrained by fewer laws—we begin to experience more freedom. This is because, in the framework we have just noted above, we are living in a

---

[297] From "The Ray of Creation," an undated study paper at *Gurdjieff and the Fourth Way: A Critical Appraisal,* a website created and curated by Douglas Staley in collaboration with Ernie Strauss. The paper can be found on-line at: <http://www.gurdjiefffourthway.org/pdf/THE%20RAY%20OF%20CREA TION.pdf> (Accessed 11/11/2020)

world closer, as it were, to the divine world or spiritual source.[298] In imaginal realms, fruits of the Spirit associate with the mystical city of Kitezh, about which we will have something more to say further below. Kitezh serves as *telos* of the "Christ people"—as a people—and as magnetic attractor.

Jesus was moving "under the radar" when he said, "Render unto Caesar what is Caesar's, and unto God what is God's." It poses a question. A similar question concerns the relation of freedom and necessity. When we elevate our vision to imagine situations and events *sub specie aeternitatis*, in light of eternity, we may begin to see that freedom and necessity are two sides of the same coin. The fact that our thoughts inherently gravitate toward the true, our actions toward the good, and our sensibility toward the beautiful, enables us to recognize a kind of "voluntary necessity" in what we think of as freedom. Our experience of freedom seems, in this way, intertwined or interlinked with the tropological. Stated another way, our experience of freedom has a moral dimension to it.

Seen from a common empirical perspective causality is linear—causes precede their effects. Seen from a larger context and more universal perspective, causality is multiple and radial—we see "connections," synchronicities, and even manifestations of the miraculous.[299] We also see, when reflecting on our own life from this larger perspective, that our life has had a kind of inner necessity to it. We see that, from this comprehensive perspective, the unfolding of our

---

[298] For a persuasive account, and fluent use and deployment, of Gurdjieff's spiritual cosmology, see Cynthia Bourgeault's *Eye of the Heart: A Spiritual Journey into the Imaginal Realm* (2020), previously cited. In her innovative interpretation of Gurdjieff's metaphysics and cosmology, the imaginal realm spans both "World 24" (the heavenly realm) and "World 48" (the physical Earth realm where we live) on the Ray of Creation. To embody "fruits of the Spirit" is to inhabit World 24, where we are under fewer laws, as well as our physical World 48. The energetic exchange along the Ray of Creation is bi-directional.

[299] With regard to causality from the larger perspective, recall the saying, "And when you threw, it was not you who threw, but God." (Qur'an 8:17) The divine wisdom is always already at work through the apparently "free" choices of humankind.

life could not have been other than it was. It is also from and through this larger perspective that the imaginal is seen to work.[300]

Leaving Babylon has many dimensions, one of which is an "inner" journey associated with a finding of the Grail, understood as a drawing near to one's Self. Alexander Mumrikov, a Russian Orthodox deacon, observed that if one carries out the Jesus Prayer properly "... one senses a kind of chalice opening upward .... The chalice represents the spiritual development of man. The first sphere is formed at the level of the chest.... The second sphere is compressed at the level of the throat. And the third sphere opens in the head."[301] Mumrikov goes on to say that the chalices depicted in Orthodox iconography "represent the science of those people who have learned how to direct their energy. They are able to feel the chalice in themselves and to watch the transformation of the energy as it takes place."[302] For Jung, according to Kingsley, the process of individuation is not individualism, but it is both the grail and quest for the grail. The process is a paradox that requires facing the abyss, surrendering oneself to the impersonal (or, in terms of this present book, the mindlessly *mechanical*).[303] In this perspective, the numinous is that (dangerous something) in the face of which you tremble.

The grail story is about the question who, or what, are you serving? Or what is life serving in you? The grail is also emblematic of the unity of Christian and pre-Christian wisdom. In legend, the grail is

---

[300] In the terminology of Gurdjieff, energies of the heavenly realm (World 24) are always breaking through into our Earthly realm (World 48) but, as we typically are—in our condition of "sleep"—we are unable to see this or to cooperate with it.

[301] From Dennis Lewis's March 1993 interview with Alexander Mumrikov in Lewis, "The Prayer of Jesus," at Lewis's website. On-line at: <https://www.dennislewis.org/articles-other-writings/articles-essays/the-prayer-of-jesus/> (Accessed 7/16/2020) See also: <https://www.dennislewis.org/articles-other-writings/articles-essays/problems/> (Accessed 7/16/2020)

[302] Ibid. For further reference to Alexander Mumrikov in context of the grail, see Glenn Friesen, *Abhishiktananda (Henri Le Saux): Christian Nondualism and Hindu Advaita* (Calgary, Canada: Aevum Books, 2015), pp. 173 ff.

[303] The divine reality is both personal and impersonal. Discernment of the personal requires the impersonal.

sometimes associated with the spear or blade.[304] Psychologically, taken together, these two images suggest both an openness to wisdom wherever we find it, to things as they are, and also a focused concentration on the task at hand. As a character in Priest-Monk Silouan's book, *Merlin on Manstone Mynd*, says, "Nothing serves the Grail except an illumined heart. It is the light that serves the Grail. … The Grail serves nothing but the glory to come, the glory that comes from above, the glory that descends when light ascends. It is glory the Grail serves."[305]

Based on his knowledge of Taoist thought, Fr. Brendan Pelphrey makes the following observations about a simple common bowl—observations which could also be made about the Grail as we seek to imagine and to understand it:

- The rim of the bowl is a circle. It has no beginning and no end.

- A bowl is a harmony, or unity. Its shape is pleasing to the eye because it is uncomplicated. It has no corners.

- A bowl is hollow (empty). If it were not hollow, it would not be a bowl. Therefore a bowl is useful not simply because of what it is, but because of what it is not.

- A bowl opens skyward. It can receive, as when we pour something into it, and it can also give, as when we pour something out of it. In this way, the capacity of a bowl is infinite, because the bowl runs over when it is full, and can be re-filled an infinite number of times. It can receive everything and it can give everything.

- A bowl is most useful to us when we do not notice it. We need it for eating rice, but then our attention is on the rice and not on the bowl itself. In fact, we scarcely notice the bowl at all.[306]

---

[304] This is a reference to the lance or spear of Longinus, the Roman centurion, that pierced the side of Jesus on the cross.

[305] Priest-Monk Silouan, *Merlin on Manstone Mynd*, (Pontesbury, Shropshire, U.K.: Stiperstones Press, 2015), p. 29.

[306] Fr. Brendan Pelphrey, "A Short Meditation on a Bowl: The *Tao Te Ching* and the Kenotic Theology of the Christian East" (1986). This article was given in slightly different form as an address to students at the Lutheran Theological Seminary/Hong Kong in 1982, and first published in Chinese and in English in *Theology and Life*, the theological journal of the Lutheran

Fr. Pelphrey finds some parallel to these observations about the ordinary bowl in themes about the Christ in Christian teaching:

- The idea of co-inherence, which the Greeks called *perichorēsis*: literally, "running the circle."
- The idea of permanent indwelling, which was called *hidrusis* (establishment), or referred to with the verb *monē* ("to dwell"), giving us the English word "remain."
- The idea of self-emptying, called *kenōsis* ("pouring out").
- The idea of external procession and openness, called *ekstasis* (literally, "standing outside"), giving us the English word "ecstasy."
- The idea of communion or self-giving love, called *koinōnia* (literally, "the many becoming one," or "communion"—not "fellowship" but literally, mystical union).

These observations blend with the understanding of the dual origins of humankind as referenced elsewhere in this present book. This blending may be discerned, imaginatively, in the following way. We may imagine the grail or cup, as a physical object—as an arising up from the Earth. The physical cup, in its empty concavity, is a *chiasmus* awaiting the descent of whatever is to be provided.[307] It waits to be filled, from the grace of heaven. To what purpose or end does the grail cup patiently wait? Its purpose is to be of service. It awaits the appearance of any and all who may be in any kind of need. We are that cup! And this is the image of reverie as process in time.

Although the Grail stories, as we first come to know them, may seem to derive from Celtic or Hiberno-British sources, we may also come to understand the legends' further associations with French, German (Teutonic), and Spanish spiritual cultures. Beyond these interconnections, we may become aware of still further inter-connections

---

Theological Seminary/Hong Kong; and later published in Danish translation. On-line at: <https://www.academia.edu/38411200/A_SHORT_MEDITATION_ON_A_BOWL_docx> (Accessed 10/28/2020). Fr. Pelphrey is a scholar and Greek Orthodox priest in Ruston, Louisiana.
307 For a paradigmatic instance of *chiasmus* in the written Word, see Bruno Barnhart's *The Good Wine: Reading John from the Center* (Eugene, Oregon: Wipf and Stock Publishers, reprint edition 2008).

within the Slavic world. Specifically, there is connection with the legends of the visible and invisible cities of Kitezh, said to be "located" in medieval central Russia, and more particularly with the bells of Kitezh. Here is a summary of one version of the story by Jason Kaminski (University of Tasmania), an Australian scholar working in cultural research:

The Kitezh story, which recounts the miraculous disappearance of a belled city beneath a lake in the face of a Mongol attack, expresses a people's will to escape from ideological domination and a totally alien world of belief, and their hope for future salvation. The narrative recounts the construction of two cities by Prince Vsevolodovich, Little Kitezh, located on the Volga River, and Great Kitezh, built alongside Little Kitezh in the Murom forest on Lake Svetloyar. In around 1236, the city of Little Kitezh is destroyed by the forces of Khan Batu, but the invating Tartars are unable to find the inner city of Great Kitezh since it is hidden away in a forest.

A fearful inhabitant of Little Kitezh (Grinshka Kuterma) betrays the way to Great Kitezh, blaming Lady Fevronia, the bride of the successor to the throne, Prince Vsevolodovich. When the Tartars arrive at the lake's edge and behold the city of Great Kitezh, a miracle occurs in answer to Kitezh's prayers for salvation to the Mother of God. The city and its entire population become invisible, apparently rising into the celestials or sinking below the lake. Seeing that God has saved the city, the Tartars flee in terror. Lady Fevronia is rewarded for her undeserved suffering by becoming a sovereign, while the traitor goes insane. The belief that the miraculous city lies beneath a lake near the Volga River draws faithful to listen through the ice of frozen lakes for the sounds of bells that are supposed to sound to this day.[308]

---

[308] Jason Kaminski, "Kolokol: Spectres of the Russian Bell," Ph.D. dissertation, University of Technology, Sydney, Australia, 2005, revised 2006, p. 29. On-line at: <https://opus.lib.uts.edu.au/bitstream/2100/421/2/02whole.pdf> (Accessed 10/6/2020). Jason Kaminski is also a composer. A focus of his current research is tantric philosophies of sound.

There are at least two reasons for calling attention to the story of Kitezh at this particular place in our narrative. These reasons have to do with the Holy Grail and with the significance of bells. These have some relevance to the topic of reverie that we are exploring in this book. First of all, it can be said that the story itself—the story of Kitezh—is a powerful and magnetic object of reverie. Some people know of Kitezh only from the 1907 Rimsky-Korsakov opera titled "The Legend of the Invisible City of Kitezh and the Maiden Fevroniya." The libretto by Vladimir Belsky was based on a conflation of two Russian legends, that of St. Fevroniya of Murom and that of the city of Kitezh, which became invisible when attacked by the Tartars.[309]

The root legends have been preserved within the Old Believer communities of itinerant Beguni-Stranniki (Runaway-Wanderer) tradition in Russia. Three separate cities of Kitezh can be identified in these legends—Little Kitezh (physical/empirical), Great Kitezh (physical/imaginal), and Great Kitezh (invisible/spiritual). The first two cities are destroyed, but all that is true, good, and beautiful about the second city is preserved in the third city, beyond any external danger. The third city is accessible to those whose hearts are attuned to it and it also serves as archetype and template for the time when Kitezh can, once again, manifest in the physical realms. This is an esoteric reading of the root legends as applicable both to societies and also to discernable levels within individual human persons.

The bells in the Kitezh legends seem relevant to this present study of reverie in that we may imagine the sound of the bells in their physicality as resounding in all three worlds—the physical, the physical/imaginal, and the invisible/spiritual. If reverie leads toward sleep, it is a particular kind or quality of sleep. It is the sleep of unknowing that allows gestation to occur, preliminary to a particular quality coming to birth within us. The sound of the bells of Kitezh is the calling forth, the welcoming of that miraculous possibility that is coming to birth. There is also another kind of sleep—the sleep of willful ignorance, of consent to the deadly sins that make it impossible

---

[309] The various strands of the Kitezh story are considered at some length in Sergei O. Prokofieff, *The Spiritual Origins of Eastern Europe and the Future Mysteries of the Holy Grail* (London: Temple Lodge, 1993) at Chapters 11-13. See also Munin Nederlander, *Kitezh: The Russian Grail Legends* (London: Aquarian Press, 1991). See also the discussion of Kitezh in my book, *The Anthropocosmic Vision*, previously cited.

for us to participate in work of the common life, the common good.[310] What serves the common good, among other things, is the presence of public intellectuals committed to a Christian humanism whose task it is to translate or to re-imagine the value of culture as a kind of education.[311]

With regard to the Holy Grail in the context of the three cities of Kitezh, the Grail can be understood as the divine-humanity, the *sobornost* or togetherness of a people living in the openness of what Rudolf Steiner has referred to as the "Grail mood." When there is failure or, more accurately, delay in manifestation of a "Christ people" the arising of a third (invisible/spiritual) city of Kitezh is necessitated in order to preserve the possibility for the later manifestation of the Kitezh qualities as a second (physical/imaginal) city and even as a first (physical/empirical) city. The Grail itself mirrors these same ontological levels in that it is a physical/empirical object, but it is also a deeply meaningful physical object that resonates from its reality in the imaginal realms. These physical manifestations of the Grail are sometimes seen and sometimes not. Beyond these physical manifestations the Grail is also an invisible/spiritual reality that is not different from the physical/imaginal reality. Whether or not the Grail manifests to a given individual has some correlation with the courage or nobility of that individual, the Grail knight. On a collective level, the Grail is the divine-humanity, considered as a single entity, that is a necessary precondition for the descent or appearance, or re-appearance in Earth, of Kitezh, the heavenly city. Conditions of our life in Babylon invite meditation on the New Testament story of Saints Paul and Silas in prison in Philippi (Acts 16:25-31). This is a story in which, by means

---

[310] This is the sleep that the Fourth Way "Work" of G. I. Gurdjieff and others is designed to resist and dispel. The writings of Maurice Nicoll, including especially his *Psychological Commentaries on the Teachings of Gurdjieff and Ouspensky* (in six volumes), *The New Man: An Interpretation of Some Parables and Miracles of Christ,* and *The Mark*, are a particularly valuable resource for recognizing and resisting this kind of "sleep."

[311] For attention to this topic in the context of post-Soviet Russia, see Vera Pozzi, "Culture as Paideia: Sergei Averintsev and Olga Sedakova: Mapping Out a Path for Contemporary Christian Humanism," *The Quarterly Journal of St. Philaret's Institute*, Issue 32, 2019. On-line at: <https://www.academia.edu/41800176/Culture_as_paideia_Sergei_Averintsev_and_Olga_Sedakova_Mapping_Out_a_Path_for_Contemporary_Christian_Humanism_in_English_> (Accessed 12/2/2020)

of an earthquake, prison shackles miraculously fall away and the door to the prison cell is miraculously unlocked. So may we discover it to be with us in our time, dear reader!

In the words of Dr. Alexander Kalomiros, who asked, "What is the profoundest characteristic of Orthodox life, the quintessential characteristic of Orthodox piety, the sign of authentic Orthodoxy as well as a premise of the true faith? It is turning inward."[312] It is a turning inward so we can, in consequence, be of service to the sacred beyond ourselves. This is the inner sense or meaning of a poetics of the Holy Grail. The Bulgarian teacher, Peter Deunov (d. 1944), said something like this: "If the poet doesn't sing or glorify the one who is truly great in the world (namely, the manifestation of Truth, Goodness, and Beauty), if the poet does not live for Him, he is not a poet. The real poet, the scientist, the preacher is only the one who glorifies this greatness, preaches it, and lives for it."[313]

In my previous books I have had occasion to refer to the possibilities enfolded within the arriving future on this planet. These possibilities have been named, variously, as the coming Age of the Holy Spirit, or the Age of Mary, or the New Epoch, or the Age of Aquarius, or the New Age.[314] The cluster of meanings is somewhat different in each of these understandings, but all these taken together reflect the intent of the heavenly beings, or of the divine cosmos, however dire the immediate and apparent circumstances may be. This intent is the restoration of all things (*apocatastasis*) and the manifest conjoining, or maximum inter-penetration, of heaven and earth. This is the long-awaited rain/rein/reign of heaven, when all eyes will be opened to see things as they are—to see our inter-relatedness on every level and at every scale. Humankind—both as a single entity and as individuals—

---

[312] As quoted at the *St. James the Just of Jerusalem Spiritual Center* website. On-line at: <http://stjamesthejust.com/> (Accessed 8/7/2020)

[313] Adapted from a talk on "The Voice of God" given by Deunov on August 26, 1930. On-line (in Bulgarian) at: <https://triangle.bg/books/1930-08-27-05.1998/1930-08-27-05.html> (Accessed 10/24/2020)

[314] In his autobiographical book, *Witness: The Story of a Search* (J. G. Bennett Foundation, 2017), John Bennett used the term, Synergic Epoch, to refer to the coming age. Much earlier, Nicholas Berdyaev wrote of the "Third Epoch" and the "Eighth Day of Creation." See selected quotes from Berdyaev on this topic, along with their textual sources, on-line at: <http://www.chebucto.ns.ca/Philosophy/Sui-Generis/Berdyaev/q8.htm> (Accessed 12/27/2020)

are tasked with participation in this process of restoration. Jacob Boehme had discerned the arriving, in his day, of "a time of the Lily." He wrote: "For a Lily blossoms upon the mountains and valleys in all the ends of the Earth: One who seeks finds. Amen. Hallelujah!"[315]

Part of what is meant by the "restoration of all things" is cultural enlightenment.[316] This requires attention to the content and quality of education that is provided to our children. If, since ancient times, democratic Greece (Athens) has seemed a pinnacle of culture, it is because its population was educated, from the time of their youth, in the values that enabled a democratic society to function. When this type of education is not provided, societies slip into populism and the failures of self-government. With regard to Ireland in the late 1950's, for example, the Irish historian, Dermot Mac Manus (d. 1990), wrote the following:

> Ireland is a land where the quiet reality of the fairies is still accepted as a matter of everyday truth, in spite of the impact of the superficialities and robotisms of today's mechanical inventions. Of course, like other people the Irish are suffering from the artificial inanities of so much of the radio and films, as well as from rushing, strident cars on our deepest country roads and nature-outraging tractors tearing up our fields. Our young people suffer from "practical" education which turns out standardized semi-educated minds—just as factories turn out cars.[317]

---

[315] As quoted in Wayne Kraus, "The Seventh Seal: The Prophecies of Jacob Boehme," Jacob Boehme Online, at: <http://jacobboehmeonline.com/yahoo_site_admin/assets/docs/The_Seventh_Seal.29072326.pdf> (Accessed 1/13/2021). As Wayne Kraus comments, "… prophecy does not expire upon fulfillment. The fulfillment of prophecy occurs not just once, but in a series of historic cycles, each fulfillment adumbrating the grand finale and each approximating it more nearly, like the waves of the sea at floe tide, each wave reaching higher up the sands."

[316] Characteristics of cultural enlightenment are discussed at some length at Section 5, "Dialogic Civilization," of my book, *The Anthropocosmic Vision*, previously cited.

[317] Dermot Mac Manus, *The Middle Kingdom: The Faerie World of Ireland* (Gerrards Cross, Buckinghamshire: Colin Smythe Limited, 1973, reprinted 1993), p. 29. The "middle kingdom" of faerie, in its presentation (or showing, revealing, or unveiling), is clearly a work of the imaginal.

In social contexts described in this way, it is no wonder that school children turn to "daydreaming" as a way out of the "box" of their school situation. Daydreaming illustrates the liberating function of reverie, a function that is subversive of dominator cultures (such as in the type of education on offer in this characterization from modern Ireland).[318] In eighteenth century Ukraine, Grigory Skovoroda (d. 1794) found his own way out of the "boxes" of his time by choosing the life of a wandering poet and philosopher. Skovoroda was a Christian sage who seems to have kept a certain distance from the official church of his day, but who nevertheless defended it. Skovoroda's life as a wandering poet and teacher was his way of escaping the confines of Babylon. He had wanted his epitaph to read: "The world tried to catch me, but it could not." We might usefully ask ourselves—in our own particular and local circumstances—what educational processes currently exist, if any, for providing our youth with the tools necessary for discerning the True, the Good, and the Beautiful? How is love for the True, the Good, and the Beautiful instilled and cultivated in our youth?

As the Irish writer and cultural philosopher, Desmond Fennell, has written, "The contemporary West is not—despite our constant calling of them to memory—built on Auschwitz and Treblinka, to which we have said 'No.' It is built on Hiroshima and Nagasaki to which we have said 'Yes.'"[319] Flowing from this, present circumstances and trends on our planet are not good.[320] This is clearly evident to all who have eyes to see. From environmental catastrophe to climate change, to economic imbalance, to viral pandemic, and the failures of justice on every possible scale, it is clear that all these interrelated phenomena are symptomatic of ways of life that cannot continue. These phenomena

---

[318] See the discussion of the expression "dominator culture" at the beginning of this section at footnote 268, page 130, above.

[319] Desmond Fennell, *The Revision of European History* (Belfast, Northern Ireland: Athol Books, 2003), p. 105.

[320] As a hopeful counterpoint to the idea of the atomic bomb as a pivotal event in Western civilization, we might remember that the historian, Arnold Toynbee (d. 1975), said that, in his opinion, the coming of the dharma to the West might well prove to be the most important event of the twentieth century. The Buddhist dharma, as received into the West, can be thought of as having a melodic quality and appeal. Melody is not entrapped by the machine!

are the result of interconnected mechanisms at the service of ego. Either humankind will disappear or something like an evolutionary or quantum leap to a new level of planetary awareness will occur—sooner rather than later.[321] It is not as if there have been no prophets or if we have had no warnings.[322] Our assigned work, in our particular time and place, is the joyful and confident work of ascension. In his book, *The Rose of the World (Roza Mira)*, Daniil Andreev, wrote of this movement into the next phase of our common life on this planet:

> The appearance of the *Rose of the World* has been preceded by the scientific era, an era that revolutionized humanity's view of the universe, of nations, of cultures, and of their fates. It has been preceded by yet another era: one of radical social changes and upheavals, of revolutions, and of world wars. Both kinds of phenomena have loosened humanity's psychological crust, which had remained for so many centuries unbroken. In that soil, plowed up by the iron teeth of historical catastrophes, the seeds of metahistorical revelation will fall. And the entire planetary cosmos will reveal itself to people's spiritual sight as a constantly evolving system of variegated worlds, a system speeding toward a blindingly brilliant goal, spiritualized and transformed from century to century and from day to day. Images from future eras are beginning to show through our reality—each in all its inimitable uniqueness, in its correlation of metahistorical forces battling within it. The collective mystical consciousness of all living humanity, it will illumine the meaning of the historical processes of the past, present, and future in order to assume creative guidance of those processes. If one may speak of any dogmas in its teaching, then those

---

[321] The term, *ecozoic*, was coined by Thomas Berry in conversation with Brian Swimme for their book, *The Universe Story: From the Primordial Flaring Forth to the Ecozoic Era—A Celebration of the Unfolding of the Cosmos* (New York: HarperCollins, 1992, 1994), to describe the geologic era that Earth is now entering—an era in which humans aspire to live in a mutually enhancing relationship with Earth and the Earth community.

[322] For just one recent example, among many possible examples, see Llewellyn Vaughan-Lee's book, *Darkening of the Light: Witnessing the End of an Era* (Point Reyes, California: The Golden Sufi Center, 2013).

dogmas will be deeply dynamic, multifaceted, and capable of further enrichment, development, and long-range evolution....

Not a hierocracy, not a monarchy, not an oligarchy, not a republic: something qualitatively different from all that has come before will emerge. It will be a global-wide social system working toward sanctifying and enlightening all life on earth. I do not know what it will be called. The point is not in the name but in the essence. Its essence will consist of work in the name of spiritualizing individuals, all of humanity, and nature.[323]

Reveriesial writing, even if manifesting in the form of prose, is not simply or merely "fiction." Bathed in the divine light, it is clear-sighted, far-seeing, and far-hearing—clairvoyant and claireaudient. It speaks a welcome to the world that is arriving—a world that is heralded by signs and wonders, seen and heard by those with eyes to see and ears to hear.[324] It is a world characterized by the Christian sage, Robert Lax, as follows:

I think we will steadily become more receptive to what love really means. There will be a collective understanding of where we came from, where we are, and where we are going. I feel that we will increasingly sense a greater interconnection and unity with the whole of existence, and so we will become more gentle, more intuitive, more caring, more giving, more loving as a result. As the love increasingly flows, I believe that we will tap into our dreams more, and, by doing that, make better sense of our lives because the unconscious and conscious states will be wonderfully linked through a palpable transfiguring love.

---

[323] From an excerpt of *The Rose of the World* on-line at: <https://1000petals.wordpress.com/2010/02/25/the-vision-the-rose-of-the-world-as-a-new-global-social-system/> (Accessed 10/26/2020). This work was begun while Andreev was incarcerated from 1947 to 1957 at Vladimir Central Prison where he experienced mystic visions. The work was finished after his release.

[324] Andreev's *Rose of the World* is an instance of reveriesial writing that is straining for a language to express a synergy among the religious traditions—a synergy that seeks to give voice to the heart of the universe. *Journey of the Universe* is a film (2013) and recent book (2020), based on collaborative work of Thomas Berry, Brian Swimme, and Mary Evelyn Tucker, that is a further expression of this intent.

The cosmos was born in joyful love, and toward joyful love we are heading.[325]

May it be so! Remember the key! It may be that as we begin to experience ourselves as living in Babylon, our choices come down to these two—whether to be a *conscious servant* or an *unconscious slave*. In one of his last books, the Irish poet, John O'Donohue (d. 2008), wrote the following lines:

> May I have the courage today
> To live the life that I would love.
> To postpone my dream no longer
> But to do at last what I came here for
> And waste my heart on fear no more.[326]

---

[325] As spoken by Robert Lax to Steve Georgiou and quoted in Steve Theodore Georgiou, *The Way of the Dreamcatcher: Spirit Lessons with Robert Lax: Poet, Peacemaker, Sage*, previously cited, p. 242. These words are also reproduced, in part, at the Lax-related website curated by Michael McGregor at <https://www.robertlax.com/robert-lax-politics/> (Accessed 11/15/2020)

[326] From "A Morning Offering" in John O'Donohue, *To Bless the Space Between Us: A Book of Blessings* (New York: Doubleday, 2008), p. 9.

11. Works and Resources Cited

Aboulker-Muskat, Colette. *Mea Culpa: Tales of Resurrection.* New York: ACMI Press, 1997.

Alexander, Christopher. *The Nature of Order: An Essay on the Art of Building and the Nature of the Universe.* Four volumes. Berkeley, California: The Center for Environmental Structure, 2005.

Alexander, Christopher. *Notes on the Synthesis of Form.* Cambridge, Massachusetts: Harvard University Press, 1964.

Almond, Ian. "The Honesty of the Perplexed: Derrida and Ibn 'Arabi on Bewilderment," *Journal of the American Academy of Religion*, Volume 70, Issue 3, September 2002, pp. 515–537. Abstract on-line at: <https://doi.org/10.1093/jaar/70.3.515> (Accessed 8/11/2020)

Amis, Robin. *A Different Christianity: Early Christian Esotericism and Modern Thought.* Albany, New York: State University of New York Press, 1995.

Andreev, Daniil. *The Rose of the World.* Hudson, New York: Lindisfarne Books, 1997. Limited excerpts on-line at: <http://www.rodon.org/andreev/trotw.htm> and at: <https://1000petals.wordpress.com/2010/02/25/the-vision-the-rose-of-the-world-as-a-new-global-social-system/> (Accessed 10/26/2020)

Anonymous. "The Wanderer," an Anglo-Saxon poem in Old English. Translated by Jeffrey Hopkins. In *VQR: A National Journal of Literature & Discussion*, Spring 1977. On-line at: < https://www.vqronline.org/essay/wanderer-anglo-saxon-poem-translated-jeffrey-hopkins> (Accessed 2/27/2021)

Anonymous. Robert Powell, translator. *Meditations on the Tarot: A Journey into Christian Hermeticism.* New York: Jeremy P. Tarcher / Putnam, 2002.

Association of Nature and Forest Therapy Guides and Programs at: <https://www.natureandforesttherapy.org/> (Accessed 7/5/2020)

Azize, Joseph. *Gurdjieff: Mysticism, Contemplation, and Exercises.* Oxford, U.K.: Oxford University Press, 2020.

Azize, Joseph. *The Phoenician Solar Theology An Investigation Into the Phoenician Opinion of the Sun Found in Julian's Hymn to King Helios.* Piscataway, New Jersey: Gorgias Press, 2005.

Azize, Joseph. "Solar Mysticism in Gurdjieff and Neoplatonism,"
    *Crossroads: An Interdisciplinary Journal for the Study of History,
    Philosophy, Religion, and Classics*, 2010, Volume 5, Issue 1, pp. 18-26,
    p. 22. On-line at: <http://www.uq.edu.au/crossroads/Archives/
    Vol%205/Issue%201%202010/Vol5Iss110%20-%204.Azize%
    20(p.18-26).pdf> (Accessed 11/11/2020)

Azize, Joseph. "Unity is the Psychological Attribute of Immortality."
    On-line at: <https://gurdjieffbooks.wordpress.com/2008/09/
    08/unity-is-the-psychological-attribute-of-immortality/>
    (Accessed 11/2/2020)

Bachelard, Gaston. *The Poetics of Reverie: Childhood, Language, and the
    Cosmos.* Boston, Massachusetts: Beacon Press, 1971.

Baghos, Mario. "Christ, Paradise, Trees, and the Cross in the
    Byzantine Art of Italy," *International Journal of Orthodox Theology*,
    2018, Volume 9, Issue 2, pp. 112-155. On-line at: <https://
    www.academia.edu/37603531/Christ_Paradise_Trees_and_the_
    Cross_in_the_Byzantine_Art_of_Italy> (Accessed 9/30/2020)

Bahnson, Fred. "The Church Forests of Ethiopia: A Mystical
    Geography," Emergence Magazine (website). On-line at:
    <https://emergencemagazine.org/story/the-church-forests-of-
    ethiopia/> (Accessed 7/24/2020)

Barks, Coleman. Performance of Rumi's poem, "Love Dogs," with
    musical accompaniment by Eugene Friesen and Arto
    Tuncboyaciyan, at one of the Mythic Journeys conferences.
     On-line at: <https://youtu.be/UF4_KZfIfVI> (Accessed
    8/28/2020)

Barnhart, Bruno. *The Good Wine: Reading John from the Center.* Eugene,
    Oregon: Wipf and Stock Publishers, reprint edition 2008.

Bashier, Salman. *Ibn al-'Arabi's Barzakh: The Concept of the Limit and the
    Relationship Between God and the World.* New York: State University
    of New York Press, 2004.

Bate, Dom Alistair OSBA. "Celtic and Benedictine—Common
    Ground?," an essay at the Holy Celtic Church International
    website. On-line at: <https://holycelticchurch.weebly.com/
    celtic--benedictine.html> (Accessed 9/7/2020)

Bauman, Lynn C.; Ward J. Bauman, and Cynthia Bourgeault. *The
    Luminous Gospels: Thomas, Mary Magdalene, and Philip.* Telephone,
    Texas: Praxis Publishing, 2008.

Bauman, Zygmunt. *Liquid Modernity.* Malden, Massachusetts: Polity
    Press, 2012.

Beal, Jenny. "The Direct Path to Happiness" (2016), at the *Ouspensky Today* website, on-line at: <https://www.ouspenskytoday.org/wp/wp-content/uploads/The-Direct-Path-to-Happiness.pdf> (Accessed 8/4/2020)

Bennett, John G. *The Dramatic Universe.* Four volumes. Reprint edition. Santa Fe, New Mexico: Bennett Books, 2018.

Bennett, John G. "The Hyperborean Origin of the Indo-European Culture," *Systematics Journal: The Journal of The Institute for the Comparative Study of History, Philosophy and the Sciences,* December 1963, Volume 1, Number 3. On-line at: <https://www.systematics.org/journal/vol1-3/SJ1-3c.htm> (Accessed 11/4/2020)

Bennett, John G. *Witness: The Story of a Search.* J. G. Bennett Foundation, 2017.

Berdyaev, Nicholas. *Freedom and the Spirit.* Oliver Fielding Clarke, translator. New York: Charles Scribner's Sons, 1935.

Berdyaev, Nikolai. Selected quotes "On the 'Third Epoch' or 'Eighth Day of Creation'" at Dirk H. Kelder's Berdyaev resources website. On-line at: <http://www.chebucto.ns.ca/Philosophy/Sui-Generis/Berdyaev/q8.htm> (Accessed 12/27/2020)

Berry, Thomas. *The Great Work: Our Way into the Future.* New York: Bell Tower / Crown, reprint edition, 2000.

Bintley, Michael D. J. *Trees in the Religions of Early Medieval England.* Woodbridge, Suffolk, U.K.: The Boydell Press, 2015.

Blake, William Blake. "Auguries of Innocence," a poem in *Poets of the English Language: Volume IV: Blake to Poe.* New York: Viking Press, 1950. Reproduced on-line at the Poetry Foundation website: <https://www.poetryfoundation.org/poems/43650/auguries-of-innocence> (Accessed 11/28/2020)

Bloom, Anthony. *Beginning to Pray.* Mahwah, New Jersey: Paulist Press, 1970.

Blue, Dana, and Caron Harrang, editors. *From Reverie to Interpretation: Transforming Thought into the Action of Psychoanalysis.* First edition. London, United Kingdom: Routledge, 2016.

Boehme, Jacob. *The Clavis.* Facsimile edition. Whitefish, Montana: Kessinger Publishing Company, no date.

Bohm, David. Lee Nichol, editor. *On Dialogue.* London: Routledge, 1996, 2004.

Bourgeault, Cynthia. *Eye of the Heart: A Spiritual Journey into the Imaginal Realm.* Boston: Shambhala, 2020.

Bourgeault, Cynthia. *The Holy Trinity and the Law of Three: Discovering the Radical Truth at the Heart of Christianity.* Boston, Massachusetts: Shambhala Publications, 2013.

Brock, Rita Nakashima, and Rebecca Ann Parker. *Saving Paradise: How Christianity Traded Love of This World for Crucifixion and Empire.* Boston: Beacon Press, 2008.

Brooke, Peter. "Nicholas Laos on Orthodoxy," an essay at Peter Brooke's website. On-line at: <http://www.peterbrooke.org/politics-and-theology/orthodoxy-index/laos.html> (Accessed 7/4/2020)

Brown, Tyson. *Abba Keddus: Rastafari and the Return of Our Sacred Origins.* Morrisville, North Carolina: Lulu.com, 2011.

Bulgakov, Sergius N. *Sophia: The Wisdom of God: An Outline of Sophiology.* Hudson, New York: Lindisfarne Press, 1993.

Burton, Linda, and Alex Whitehead, editors. *Christ is the Morning Star: When Celtic Spirituality meets the Benedictine Rule.* Dublin, Ireland: Lindisfarne Books, 1999.

Busch, Fred. "Searching for the analyst's reveries," *The International Journal of Psychoanalysis*, Volume 99, Number 3, 2018, pp. 569-589. On-line at: <https://sps.wildapricot.org/resources/Documents/Busch,%20Searching%20for%20the%20analyst's%20reveries.pdf> (Accessed 6/22/2020)

Camosy, Charles. "Ask Charlie Anything," short videos on animal welfare and vegetarian diet as spiritual practice. On-line at: <https://www.charlescamosy.com/ask-charlie-anything> (Accessed 7/20/2020)

Cavarnos, Constantine. *The Hellenic-Christian Philosophical Tradition.* Belmont, Massachusetts: Institute for Byzantine and Modern Greek Studies, 1989.

Chakravarty, K. Gandhar. "Rastafari Revisited: A Four-Point Orthodox/Secular Typology," *Journal of the American Academy of Religion*, March 2015, Volume 83, Issue 1, pp. 151–180. On-line at: <https://doi.org/10.1093/jaarel/lfu084> (Accessed 7/25/2020)

Chittick, William C. *The Sufi Doctrine of Rumi: Illustrated Edition.* Bloomington, Indiana: World Wisdom, 2005.

Christie, Douglas E. "Practicing Paradise: Contemplative Awareness and Ecological Renewal," *Anglican Theological Review*, Volume 94, Number 2, 2012, pp. 281-303. On-line at: <https://digitalcommons.lmu.edu/theo_fac/109/> (Accessed 8/14/2020)

Clement of Alexandria. *The Stromata, or Miscellanies*, in Alexander Roberts and James Donaldson, editors, *Ante-Nicene Fathers*, Volume 2 (Edinburgh: T&T Clark / Grand Rapids, MI: Wm. B. Eerdmans Publishing Company, reprinted 2001). On-line at the Christian Classics Ethereal Library at: <https://ccel.org/ccel/schaff/anf02/anf02/Page_305.html> (Accessed 11/19/2020)

Clement of Alexandria. *The Stromata*, in *The Catholic Encyclopedia*. On-line at: <https://www.newadvent.org/fathers/02105.htm> (Accessed 12/2/2020)

Consiglio, Cyprian. Untitled article at his website, July 11, 2005. On-line at: <http://www.cyprianconsiglio.com/5533> (Accessed 12/7/2020)

Corbin, Henry. Ruth Horine, translator from the French. *"Mundus Imaginalis* or the Imaginary and the Imaginal,"* Spring*, 1972, Zurich, Switzerland. On-line at: <http://www.bahaistudies.net/asma/mundus_imaginalis.pdf> (Accessed 6/22/2020)

de Mello S.J., Anthony. *Awareness: A de Mello Spirituality Conference in His Own Words*. New York: Doubleday, 1992. On-line at: <http://www.arvindguptatoys.com/arvindgupta/tonyawareness.pdf> (Accessed 10/31/2020)

de Souzenelle, Annick. *The Body and its Symbolism: A Kabbalistic Approach*. Translated from the French by Christopher Chaplin and Tony James. Wheaton, Illinois: Quest Books / Theosophical Publishing House, 2015.

del Valle-Inclan, Ramon. Robert Lima, translator. *The Lamp of Marvels: Aesthetic Meditations*. West Stockbridge, Massachusetts: Lindisfarne Press, 1986.

Deunov, Peter. "The Voice of God," a talk given on August 26, 1930. On-line (in Bulgarian) at: <https://triangle.bg/books/1930-08-27-05.1998/1930-08-27-05.html> (Accessed 10/24/2020)

Domin, Hilde. "Passing Landscape," a poem in English translation by Meg Taylor and Elke Heckel. On-line at: <http://hildedomin.megtaylor.co.uk/translations-1#PassingLandscape> (Accessed 9/13/2020)

Domínguez-Rosado, Brenda. *Sufism as Lorna Goodison's Alternative Poetic Path to Hope and Healing*. Newcastle upon Tyne, U.K.: Cambridge Scholars Publishing, 2019.

Drpić, Ivan. "The Enkolpion: Object, Agency, Self," in *Gesta*, Volume 57, Number 2, Fall 2018. On-line at: <https://doi.org/ 10.1086/698842> (Accessed 2/25/2021)

Dupuche, John R. "Towards a Christian Tantra: The Interplay of Christianity and Kashmir Shaivism," p. 78. On-line at: <https:// repository.divinity.edu.au/1628/1/Towards_a_Christian_Tantra. _for_Antoine_Serval-1.pdf> (Accessed 5/31/2020)

Earth Charter. Text and context, on-line: <https://earthcharter. org/> (Accessed 1/24/2021)

Eisler, Riane. *The Chalice and the Blade: Our History, Our Future.* New York: HarperCollins, 1987.

Eliot, T. S. "Burnt Norton" (No. 1 of "Four Quartets). On-line at: <http://www.davidgorman.com/4quartets/1-norton.htm> (Accessed 6/29/2020)

Emerging Earth Community. A network and resource. On-line at: <http://emergingearthcommunity.org/> (Accessed 1/24/2021)

Emory-Moore, Christopher. "Clear and Uncreated: The Experience of Inner Light in Gelug-pa Tantrism and Byzantine Hesychasm," *Buddhist-Christian Studies*, Volume 36, 2016, pp. 117-131.

Epstein, Gerald, and Barbara L. Fedoroff, editors. *The Encyclopedia of Mental Imagery: Colette Aboulker-Muscat's 2,100 Visualizations for Personal Development, Healing, and Self-knowledge.* New York, New York: ACMI Press, 2012.

Fennell, Desmond. *The Revision of European History.* Belfast, Northern Ireland: Athol Books, 2003.

Flanagan, Bernadette, and Michael O'Sullivan. "Spirituality in Contemporary Ireland: Manifesting Indigeneity," *Spiritus: A Journal of Christian Spirituality*, Volume 16, Number 2A, Fall 2016, pp. 55-73. On-line at: <https://www.researchgate.net/ publication/314241050_Spirituality_in_Contemporary_ Ireland_Manifesting_Indigeneity> (Accessed 9/8/2020)

Freeman, Fr. Stephen. "Nostalgia for Paradise" (Kalomiros excerpt), *Glory to God for All Things* blog, February 15, 2014. On-line at: <https://blogs.ancientfaith.com/glory2godforallthings/2014/02 /15/nostalgia-for-paradise/> (Accessed 8/7/2020)

Friesen, Glenn. *Abhishiktananda (Henri Le Saux): Christian Nondualism and Hindu Advaita.* Calgary, Canada: Aevum Books, 2015.

Forsythe, Dennis. *Rastafari: For the Healing of the Nations.* New York: One Drop Books, 1999.

Full of Grace and Truth blog. Various dates. Entries concerned with animals at: <http://full-of-grace-and-truth.blogspot.com/search/label/Animals> (Accessed 8/15/2020)

Gabriel, Douglas. "Scythianos – the Hidden Master" (e-book). On-line at: <https://neoanthroposophy.files.wordpress.com/2020/03/scythianos-hidden-master_douglas-gabriel.pdf> (Accessed 10/24/2020)

Gebser, Jean. Noel Barstad with Algis Mickunas, translators. *The Ever-Present Origin*. Athens, Ohio: Ohio University Press, 1986.

Georgiou, S. T. *Mystic Street: Meditations on a Spiritual Path*. Ottawa, Canada: Novalis, 2007.

Georgiou, Steve Theodore. *The Way of the Dreamcatcher: Spirit Lessons with Robert Lax: Poet, Peacemaker, Sage*. Ottawa, Canada: Novalis, 2002.

Goodison, Lorna. Biographical entry at *The Poetry Archive*. On-line at: <https://poetryarchive.org/poet/lorna-goodison/> (Accessed 8/16/2020)

Gorski, Philip. *Goodseekers: Essays on Literature and Spirituality, East and West*. Sherwood Rise, Nottingham, U.K.: The AlphaOmega Press, 2019.

Greene, Herman. "The Long View: Thomas Berry's Instruction on the Reform of Religion, Law, and Culture in His Later Books," Center for Ecozoic Studies, website post, undated. On-line at: <https://www.ecozoicstudies.org/reviews/the-long-view-thomas-berrys-instruction-on-the-reform-of-religion-law-and-culture-in-his-later-books/> (Accessed 1/23/2021)

Gregory of Nyssa. Abraham J. Malherbe and Everett Ferguson, editors. *The Life of Moses*. The Classics of Western Spirituality. Mahwah, New Jersey: Paulist Press, 1978.

Grigoryeva, Nadezhda. "Speak Heart…: Vladimir Sorokin's Mystical Language," in Tine Roesen & Dirk Uffelmann, editors, *Vladimir Sorokin's Languages*. Volume 11 in the *Slavica Bergensia* series. University of Bergen, 2013. On-line at: <https://boap.uib.no/books/sb/catalog/view/9/8/163-1> (Accessed 2/25/2021)

Gurdjieff, G. I. *Beelzebub's Tales to His Grandson: All and Everything, First Series*. New York: Penguin Compass, 1999.

Hart, Br. Aidan. "Icons and the Material World," an address given at Iona, Scotland, September 28, 2000. On-line at: <https://aidanharticons.com/wp-content/uploads/2012/08/ICONSMAT.pdf> (Accessed 6/6/2020)

Harvey, Andrew. *The Direct Path: Creating a Personal Journey to the Divine Using the World's Spiritual Traditions.* New York: Broadway Books, 2000.

Harvey, Andrew. Video conversation between Andrew Harvey and Scott Catamas, June 2020. On-line at: <https://youtu.be/DAAX4glqXaQ> (Accessed 7/20/2020)

Hilarion of Volokolamsk, Metropolitan. "St. Symeon the New Theologian and his Teaching on the Vision of the Divine Light," *European Journal for Philosophy of Religion,* Summer 2015, Volume 7, Number 2, pp. 3-20

Hesova, Zora. "The Notion of Illumination in the Perspective of Ghazali's Mishkat al-Anwar," *Journal of Islamic Thought and Civilization,* Volume 2, Issue 2, Fall 2012, pp. 65-85. On-line at: <https://journals.umt.edu.pk/index.php/JITC/article/view/334> (Accessed 8/13/2020)

Heyneman, Martha. "Bees of the Invisible World," *Parabola,* Fall 2005, Volume 30, Number 3.

Hillman, James. T. Moore, editor. *A Blue Fire: Selected Writings by James Hillman.* New York: HarperPerennial, 1991.

Hooke, Della. *Trees in Anglo-Saxon England: Literature, Lore and Landscape.* Woodbridge, Suffolk, U.K.: The Boydell Press, 2010.

Horgan, John. "Was Psychedelic Guru Terence McKenna Goofing About 2012 Prophecy?," *Scientific American* blog, June 6, 2012. On-line at: <https://blogs.scientificamerican.com/cross-check/was-psychedelic-guru-terence-mckenna-goofing-about-2012-prophecy/> (Accessed 11/22/2020)

Hunt, Hannah. *A Guide to St. Symeon the New Theologian.* Eugene, Oregon: Wipf and Stock / Cascade Books, 2015.

Ibn Yusuf, Ya'qub. "The Archetype of the Tzaddiq in Hasidic Tradition." Master's thesis, University of Manitoba, 1992. On-line at: <http://mspace.lib.umanitoba.ca/bitstream/1993/18558/1/Ibn_Yusif_The_archetype.pdf> (Accessed 7/27/2020)

Introvigne, Massimo. "Between 'Essence Religion' and 'Godly Religion': The Italian Communal Esotericism of the Universal Soul Movement," a paper presented at the North American Conference on Esotericism, Michigan State University, Kellogg Center, June 3-6, 2004. Published on-line at *CESNUR: Center for Studies on New Religions.* <https://www.cesnur.org/2004/mi_essence.htm> (Accessed 9/5/2020)

Johnson, Jeremy D. *Seeing Through the World: Jean Gebser and Integral Consciousness.* Seattle, Washington: Revelore Press, 2019.

Jung, Carl. *Psychology and Alchemy.* Volume 12 in the *Collected Works of C. G. Jung*, Bollingen Series. Princeton, New Jersey: Princeton University Press, 1968, 1980.

Kalomiros, Alexander. *Nostalgia for Paradise.* English edition. Ridgewood, New Jersey: Zephyr Publishing, 2006.

Kalomiros, Alexander. "The River of Fire"

Kaminski, Jason. "Kolokol: Spectres of the Russian Bell," Ph.D. dissertation, University of Technology, Sydney, Australia, 2005, revised 2006, p. 29. On-line at: <https://opus.lib.uts.edu.au/ bitstream/2100/421/2/02whole.pdf> (Accessed 10/6/2020)

Kapstein, Matthew T. Editor. *The Presence of Light: Divine Radiance and Religious Experience.* Chicago: University of Chicago Press, 2004.

Kardong, Terrence G. *The Life of St. Benedict by Gregory the Great: Translation and Commentary.* Collegeville, Minnesota: Liturgical Press, 2009.

Khan, Pir Vilayat Inayat. *Awakening: A Sufi Experience.* New York: Jeremy P. Tarcher / Putnam, 1999.

Kharitidi, Olga. *Master of Lucid Dreams.* Charlottesville, Virginia: Hampton Roads Publishing Company, 2001.

Kilcourse, George. "'The Paradise Ear': Thomas Merton, Poet," *The Kentucky Review*, Summer 1987, Volume 7, Number 2, Article 8, pp. 98-121.

Kingsley, Peter. *A Story Waiting to Pierce You: Mongolia, Tibet and the Destiny of the Western World.* Point Reyes, California: Golden Sufi Center Publishing, 2010.

Kingsley, Peter, and Adyashanti. *Being Unlimited* podcast, June 25, 2020. On-line at: <https://beingunlimited.org/being-rooted-in-the-eternal-with-peter-kingsley> (Accessed 8/12/2020)

Kingsley, Peter. *In the Dark Places of Wisdom.* Point Reyes, California: Golden Sufi Center Publishing, 1999.

Knysh, Alexander D. *Sufism: A New History of Islamic Mysticism.* Princeton, New Jersey: Princeton University Press, 2017.

Koroleva, Larissa. "Daniil Andreev: *The Mythology of The Rose of the World*," 2002, Ph.D. dissertation, University of New South Wales (Australia). On-line at: <https://www.unsworks.unsw.edu.au/ primo-explore/fulldisplay/unsworks_64362/UNSWORKS> (Accessed 10/29/2020)

Kotte, Dieter; Qing Li; Won Sop Shin; and Andreas Michalsen, editors. *International Handbook of Forest Therapy*. Newcastle upon Tyne, U.K.: Cambridge Scholars Publishing, 2019. Publisher's description at: <https://www.cambridgescholars.com/international-handbook-of-forest-therapy> (Accessed 7/5/2020)

Kraus, Wayne. "The Seventh Seal: The Prophecies of Jacob Boehme, "Jacob Boehme Online, at: <http://jacobboehmeonline.com/yahoo_site_admin/assets/docs/The_Seventh_Seal.29072326.pdf> (Accessed 1/13/2021).

Kripal, Jeffrey J. *The Flip: Epiphanies of Mind and the Future of Knowledge*. New York: Bellevue Literary Press, 2019.

Lampert, Evgueny. *Nicolas Berdyaev and the New Middle Ages*. London: James Clarke & Co., Ltd., [1945].

Laos, Nicolas. *The Hesychastic Illuminism and the Theory of the Third Light*. London: White Crane Publishing, 2014.

Lavriotis, Maximos. "St. Maximus' cosmology and modern astrophysics," September 19, 1998. On-line at: <https://digilander.libero.it/gogmagog1/ortodossia/Cosmology.htm> (Accessed 6/14/2020)

Lax, Robert. *Circus Days and Nights*. New York: The Overlook Press, Peter Mayer Publishers, Inc., 2000.

Lax, Robert. James J. Uebbing, editor. *Love had a Compass*. New York: Grove Press, 1996.

Leloup, Jean-Yves. *Judas and Jesus: Two Faces of a Single Revelation*. Joseph Rowe, translator. Rochester, Vermont: Inner Traditions, 2007.

Leneghan, Francis. "Preparing the Mind for Prayer: *The Wanderer*, *hesychasm* and *theosis*," *Neophilologus*, 2015. On-line at: <https://link.springer.com/article/10.1007%2Fs11061-015-9455-3> (Accessed 2/27/2021)

Leon-Portilla, Miguel. *Aztec Thought and Culture: A Study of the Ancient Nahuatl Mind*. Revised edition. Jack Emory Davis, translator. Norman, Oklahoma: University of Oklahoma Press, 1963.

Lermontov, Mikhail. "The Angel" (1831). A poem in English translation, as reproduced in Christopher Bamford's Introduction to Nikolai Berdyaev, *The Russian Idea*. Hudson, New York: Lindisfarne Press, 1992.

Lewis, Dennis. "The Prayer of Jesus," containing an interview with Alexander Mumrikov, at Lewis's website. On-line at: <https://www.dennislewis.org/articles-other-writings/articles-essays/the-prayer-of-jesus/> (Accessed 7/16/2020). See also: <https://www.dennislewis.org/articles-other-writings/articles-essays/problems/> (Accessed 7/16/2020)

Llewelyn, Robert. *A Doorway to Silence: Contemplative Use of the Rosary.* London: Darton, Longman and Todd, 1986.

Llewelyn, Robert. "Introducing a Rosary of Peace," brief notes. On-line at: <http://www.annunciationtrust.org.uk/prayercards/Introducing%20A%20Rosary%20of%20Peace.pdf> (Accessed 11/16/2020)

Lombardi, Riccardo. "Time, Music, and Reverie," *Journal of the American Psychoanalytic Association*, Volume 54, Issue 4, December 1, 2008, pp. 1191-1211. Information on-line at: <https://doi.org/10.1177%2F0003065108326107> (Accessed 1/10/2021)

Louth, Andrew. *Maximus the Confessor.* New York: Routledge, 1996.

Louth, Fr. Andrew. "Maximus the Confessor and Modern Science," a lecture, undated. Via a blog post by Macrina Walker, "The human person as priest of the cosmos," at the blog, *A Vow of Conversation*, April 30, 2009. On-line at: <https://avowofconversation.wordpress.com/2009/04/30/the-human-person-as-priest-of-the-cosmos/> (Accessed 6/7/2020)

Mac Manus, Dermot. *The Middle Kingdom: The Faerie World of Ireland.* Gerrards Cross, Buckinghamshire: Colin Smythe Limited, 1973, reprinted 1993.

Markides, Kyriacos C. "Eastern Orthodox Mysticism and Transpersonal Theory," *The Journal of Transpersonal Psychology*, Volume 40, Number 2, Fall 2008, pp. 178-198 On-line at: <https://pdfs.semanticscholar.org/9bcb/f3c9735a53a280e420c4465fc1bc680df0d9.pdf> (Accessed 1/21/2021)

Mathew, Marilyn. "Reverie: between thought and prayer," July 2005, *Journal of Analytical Psychology*, Volume 50, Number 3, pp. 383-93. Abstract on-line at: <https://www.researchgate.net/publication/7814997_Reverie_between_thought_and_prayer> (Accessed 9/15/2020

Matus, Thomas. *Yoga and the Jesus Prayer.* Winchester, U.K.: John Hunt Publishing / O Books, 2010.

Maurin, Peter. *Easy Essays.* Eugene, Oregon: Wipf and Stock Publishers, 2010; previously published by Rose Hill Books, 2003.

Maximus the Confessor. *Maximus Confessor: Selected Writings.* Translated by George C. Berthold; Introduction by Jaroslav Pelikan; and Preface by Irénée-Henri Dalmais, O.P. Mahwah, New Jersey: Paulist Press, 1985.

McCullough, Glenn J. "Jacob Boehme and the Spiritual Roots of Psychodynamic Psychotherapy: Dreams, Ecstasy, and Wisdom," Ph.D. dissertation, Toronto School of Theology, University of St. Michael's College, 2019. On-line at: <https://tspace.library. utoronto.ca/handle/1807/99728> (Accessed 2/27/2021)

McGregor, Michael N. *Pure Act: The Uncommon Life of Robert Lax.* New York: Fordham University Press, 2015.

McGuckin, John. "Symeon the New Theologian's *Hymns of Divine Eros*: A Neglected Masterpiece of the Christian Mystical Tradition," *Spiritus*, 5 (2005): 182–202, p. 182. On-line at: <https:// academiccommons.columbia.edu/download/fedora_content/ download/ac:146165/content/5.2mcguckin.pdf> (Accessed 6/4/2020)

Mastilovic, Stefan. "A Never-Ending Story? The 'Age of the Fathers,' St. Symeon the New Theologian's Notion of Patristic Authority, and the Church Fathers of Modern Times," Bachelor of Theology (Honours) thesis, Sydney College of Divinity, St. Andrew's Greek Orthodox Theologian College, 2014, p. 45. On-line at: <https://www.academia.edu/34410511/A_NEVER_ ENDING_STORY_The_Age_of_the_Fathers_St_Symeon_the_ New_Theologian_s_Notion_of_Patristic_Authority_and_the_ Church_Fathers_of_Modern_Times> (Accessed 1/7/2021)

Mehl-Madrona, Lewis. *Healing the Mind through the Power of Story: The Promise of Narrative Psychiatry.* Rochester, Vermont: Bear & Company, 2010.

Mehl-Madrona, Lewis. *Narrative Medicine: The Use of History and Story in the Healing Process.* Rochester, Vermont: Bear & Company, 2007.

Meier, Carl. A. *Healing Dream and Ritual: Ancient Incubation and Modern Psychotherapy.* 4th edition. Einsiedeln, Switzerland: Daimon Verlag, 2009.

Merton, Thomas. *The Way of Chuang Tzu.* New York: New Directions Publishing, 1997.

Milarepa. Garma C. C. Chang, translator. *The Hundred Thousand Songs of Milarepa*. Reprint edition. New York: Harper Colophon, 1970. Selected songs on-line at: <http://www.kreisels.com/milarepa/milarepa-songs-english.htm> (Accessed 9/12/2020)

Moriarty, John. *Dreamtime*. Dublin, Ireland: The Lilliput Press, 2020.

Mouravieff, Boris. Robin Amis, editor. *Gnosis: Study and Commentaries on the Esoteric Tradition of Eastern Orthodoxy*. Three volumes. Shaftesbury, U.K.: Praxis Institute Press / Agora Books, 1990, 1992, 1993.

"Music of the Ainur." Essay at the Tolkien Gateway. On-line at: <http://tolkiengateway.net/wiki/Music_of_the_Ainur> (Accessed 12/27/2020)

Naumescu, Vlad. "Learning the 'Science of Feelings': Religious Training in Eastern Christian Monasticism," *Ethnos: Journal of Anthropology*, Volume 77, Number 2, 2012, pp. 227-251. On-line at: <https://www.tandfonline.com/doi/full/10.1080/00141844.2011.595809> (Accessed 7/25/2020)

Nederlander, Munin. *Kitezh: The Russian Grail Legends*. London: Aquarian Press, 1991.

Needleman, Jacob. *Lost Christianity: A Journey of Rediscovery*. New York: TarcherPerigee (reprint edition), 2003.

Nichol, Lee. Editor. *The Essential David Bohm*. London: Routledge / Taylor & Francis e-Library, 2005.

Nicodemos of the Holy Mountain. *A Handbook of Spiritual Counsel*. Classics of Western Spirituality series. Mahwah, New Jersey: Paulist Press, 1988.

Nicoll, Maurice. *The Mark*. Boston & Boulder: Shambhala Publications, 1955/1981. On-line at: <https://selfdefinition.org/gurdjieff/maurice-nicoll-directory/Maurice-Nicoll-The-Mark-1953.pdf> (Accessed 10/11/2020)

Nicoll, Maurice. *The New Man: An Interpretation of Some Parables and Miracles of Christ*. Boston & Boulder: Shambhala Publications, 1950. On-line at: <https://selfdefinition.org/gurdjieff/maurice-nicoll-directory/Maurice-Nicoll-The-New-Man.pdf> (Accessed 10/11/2020)

Nicoll, Maurice. *Psychological Commentaries on the Teachings of Gurdjieff and Ouspensky*. In six volumes. York Beach, Maine: Samuel Weiser, 1996. On-line at: <https://selfdefinition.org/gurdjieff/maurice-nicoll-directory/> (Accessed 10/11/2020)

Nottingham, Rebecca. *The Work: Esotericism and Christian Psychology.* Independently published, 2018.

Nouwen, Henri J. M. *Behold the Beauty of the Lord: Praying with Icons.* Notre Dame, Indiana: Ave Maria Press, 1987.

O'Donohue, John. *To Bless the Space Between Us: A Book of Blessings.* New York: Doubleday, 2008.

O'Leary, Peter. "An imaginal homage to Joseph Donahue," undated essay at *Jacket 2* website. On-line at: <https://jacket2.org/article/imaginal-homage-joseph-donahue> (Accessed 11/9/2020)

Ouspensky, P. D. *In Search of the Miraculous.* New York: Harcourt Brace Jovanovich, 1949.

Papademetriou, George C. "The Enlightenment of Zen Buddhism and the Hesychastic Vision of the Divine Light," *Journal of Ecumenical Studies*, Volume 50, Issue 1, Winter 2015, p. 57. On-line at: <https://www.academia.edu/37538311/the_enlightenment_of_zen_buddhism_and_the_hesychastic_vision_of_the_divine_light> (Accessed 1/7/2021)

Papanagiotou, Efstratios. *Spiritual Metamorphosis: The Awakening of the Human Heart.* Second Edition. [Indianapolis, Indiana]: Theosis Books, 2013.

Papanagiotou, Efstratios. *Divinization: The Hidden Teaching Within Divine Wisdom.* Second Edition. [Indianapolis, Indiana]: Theosis Books, 2013.

Papanagiotou, Efstratios. *The Inner Restoration of Christianity.* Second Edition. [Indianapolis, Indiana]: Theosis Books, 2013.

Pelphrey, Fr. Brendan. "A Short Meditation on a Bowl: The *Tao Te Ching* and the Kenotic Theology of the Christian East," *Theology and Life*, theological journal of the Lutheran Theological Seminary/Hong Kong, 1986. On-line at: <https://www.academia.edu/38411200/A_SHORT_MEDITATION_ON_A_BOWL_docx> (Accessed 10/28/2020)

Perlo, Katherine Wills. *Kinship and Killing: The Animal in World Religions.* New York: Columbia University Press, 2009.

Pozzi, Vera. "Culture as Paideia: Sergei Averintsev and Olga Sedakova: Mapping Out a Path for Contemporary Christian Humanism," *The Quarterly Journal of St. Philaret's Institute*, Issue 32, 2019. On-line at: <https://www.academia.edu/41800176/Culture_as_paideia_Sergei_Averintsev_and_Olga_Sedakova_Mapping_Out_a_Path_for_Contemporary_Christian_Humanism_in_English_> (Accessed 12/2/2020)

Priest-Monk Silouan. *Merlin on Manstone Mynd.* Pontesbury, Shropshire, U.K.: Stiperstones Press, 2015.

Priest-Monk Silouan, "Wisdom Centuries," at Wisdom Hermitage website. On-line at: <http://www.wisdomhermitage.org.uk/wisdom-songs-2011/> (Accessed 6/2/2020)

Prokofieff, Sergei O. *The Spiritual Origins of Eastern Europe and the Future Mysteries of the Holy Grail.* London: Temple Lodge, 1993.

Pushkin, Alexander. Untitled 8-verse poem from 1829. As translated/adapted by Peter Bird. On-line at: <http://peterbird.name/choral/Pushkins_Reverie/Pushkins_Reverie.html> (Accessed 11/12/2020)

Raboteau, Emily. *Searching for Zion: The Quest for Home in the African Diaspora.* New York: Atlantic Monthly Press, 2013.

Ramfos, Stelios. "Inconceivable Nothingness: The Philokalia and the roots of modern Greek Nihilism: An essay in philosophical anthropology." An English translation. On-line at: <https://www.academia.edu/24236505/Inconceivable_Nothingness> (Accessed 6/23/2020)

Ramfos, Stelios. "The Secret Jesus." An English translation. On-line at: <https://www.academia.edu/24236489/THE_JESUS_SECRET> (Accessed 6/25/2020)

Ras Red Lion. "Birth of the Redeemer: Emperor Haile Selassie I," Rastafari Coalition website, July 19, 2019. On-line at: <https://www.rastafaricoalition.org/articles/redeemer.htm> (Accessed 10/16/2020)

Ravetz, Amanda. "Sipping Water: Reverie and Improvisation," *Critical Studies in Improvisation / Études critiques en improvisation*, 2012, Volume 8, Number 2. On-line at: <https://www.criticalimprov.com/index.php/csieci/article/view/2139/2924> (Accessed 9/15/2020)

Redington, Norman Hugh. "A Sketch of Rastafari History," The Saint Pachomius Library, 1995. On-line at: <http://www.voskrese.info/spl/rasta-hist.html> (Accessed 7/3/2020)

Romanyshyn, Robert D. "On Angels and Other Anomalies of the Imaginal Life," London, 2003. On-line at: <http://www. robertromanyshyn.com/files/documents/On-Angels-and-Other-Anomalies-of-the-Imaginal-Life.pdf> (Accessed 1/11/2021)

Romanyshyn, Robert D. "The Metaphor or Alchemy and the Alchemy of Metaphor: Working in the Space between Presence and Absence," April 24, 2009, on-line at: <http://www. robertromanyshyn.com/files/documents/The-Metaphor-of-Alchemy-and-the-Alchemy-of-Metaphor.pdf> (Accessed 12/13/2020)

Rossi, Vincent. "Uncreated Peace: The 'Peace that passeth all understanding' according to the *Philokalia*," *Sophia: The Journal of Traditional Studies*, Volume 9, Number 1, Summer 2003. On-line at: <https://www.academia.edu/11378867/Uncreated_Peace_the_Peace_that_passeth_all_understanding_according_to_the_Philokalia> (Accessed 7/4/2020)

Rusch, Neil. "Honey Song: What the bees—and the Bushmen— know," *Parabola*, Volume 43, Number 3. On-line at: <https:// parabola.org/2018/07/28/honey-song-by-neil-rusch/> (Accessed 10/1/2020)

Sabo, Theodore. "The Proto-Hesychasts: Origins of mysticism in the Eastern church," 2012, Ph.D. dissertation in Theology, North-West University (Potchefstroom Campus), South Africa. On-line at: <https://dspace.nwu.ac.za/bitstream/handle/10394/8218/Sabo_T.pdf> (Accessed 11/7/2020)

St. Basil the Great. Homilies for Lent, in J. P. Migne, *Patrologia graeca*. The Greek and an English translation can be found on-line at: <https://bible.org/seriespage/appendix-1-basil%e2%80%99s-sermons-about-fasting> (Accessed 10/9/2020)

St. John of the Cross. *The Dark Night of the Soul.* Translated and introduced by Mirabai Starr. New York: Riverhead Books, 2002.

St. Nikolai of Ochrid and Zica. *Prayers by the Lake.* On-line at: <http://www.sv-luka.org/praylake/index.htm> (Accessed 11/12/2020)

"St. Seraphim of Sarov's Conversation with Nicholas Motovilov: A Wonderful Revelation to the World," on-line at: <http:// orthodoxinfo.com/praxis/wonderful.aspx> (Accessed 1/3/2021)

Saint-Exupéry, Antoine de. Katherine Woods, translator. *The Little Prince*. New York: Reynal & Hitchcock, 1943. On-line at: <http://blogs.ubc.ca/edcp508/files/2016/02/TheLittlePrince.pdf> (Accessed 11/23/2020)

Saint Gregory the Great. *The Dialogues, Book Two: Life of Benedict*. On-line at: <http://archive.osb.org/gen/greg> (Accessed 1/16/2021)

Saint Symeon the New Theologian. *Hymns Of Divine Love*. Fr. George A. Maloney, translator. Denville, New Jersey: Dimension Books, 1975.

Salman, Harrie. "The Prophetic *Bylina* and the Russian Mission," in *Starlight: Journal of the Sophia Foundation*, Easter 2020, Volume 20, Number 1, pp. 41-49, pp. 17-48. On-line at: <https://sophiafoundation.org/wp-content/uploads/2020/04/Starlight-Easter-2020-issue-99p.pdf> (Accessed 10/27/2020)

Santillana, Giorgio de, and Hertha von Dechend. *Hamlet's Mill: An Essay Investigating the Origins of Human Knowledge and its Transmission Through Myth*. Jaffrey, New Hampshire: David R. Godine, Publisher /Nonpareil Books, 1969, 1977.

Sardello, Robert. *Heartfulness*. La Veta, Colorado: Goldenstone Press, 2017.

Sardello, Robert. "The Truth of the Way Down," May 23, 2020, a blog entry at his website. On-line at: <http://www.robertsardello.com/blog/may-23rd-2020> (Accessed 7/1/2020)

Scholes, Robert E. *Fabulation and Metafiction*. Urbana, Illinois: University of Illinois Press, 1979.

Scott, Ernest. *The People of the Secret*. London: Octagon Press, 1985.

Sedakova, Olga. "The Light of Life: Some Remarks on the Russian Orthodox Perception," July/August 2005, essay, at her website. On-line at: <http://www.olgasedakova.com/eng/Moralia/270> (Accessed 11/13/2020)

Sellassie, Abba Yahudah Berhan. Vik Slen, editor. *A Journey to the Roots of Rastafari: The Essene Nazarite Link*. Emeryville, California: WordSword Publishing, 2013.

Shaw, Martin. *Courting the Wild Twin*. White River Junction, Vermont: Chelsea Green Publishing, 2020.

Shuebrook, Kyle J. "Science and Sufism: A Discussion of David Bohm and Ibn al-'Arabi." Undated paper in development. On-line at: <https://www.academia.edu/2272891/Science_and_ Sufism_A_Discussion_of_David_Bohm_and_Ibn_al_Arabi> (Accessed 8/10/2020)

Sibert, Karen Sullivan. "Khourieh Randa decodes the language of icons," *aPennedPoint* website, November 5, 2019. On-line at: <https://apennedpoint.com/khourieh-randa-decodes-the-language-of-icons/> (Accessed 5/31/2020)

Sigrist, Bishop Seraphim. *Theology of Wonder.* Crestwood, New York: St. Vladimir's Seminary Press, 1999.

Smoley, Richard S. *Inner Christianity: A Guide to the Esoteric Tradition.* Boston, Massachusetts: Shambhala Publications, 2002. As reproduced on-line, without pagination, at: <https://archive. org/stream/InnerChristianityByRichardSmoley/Inner%20 Christianity%20by%20Richard%20Smoley_djvu.txt> (Accessed 6/7/2020)

Spencer, William David. *Dread Jesus.* Eugene, Oregon: Wipf and Stock, 2011.

Staley, Douglas, and Ernie Strauss. "Evolution." An undated study paper at the website, *Gurdjieff and the Fourth Way: A Critical Appraisal.* On-line at: <http://www.gurdjiefffourthway.org/pdf/ EVOLUTION.pdf> (Accessed 8/4/2020)

Staley, Douglas, and Ernie Strauss. "The Ray of Creation," An undated study paper at the website, *Gurdjieff and the Fourth Way: A Critical Appraisal.* On-line at: <http://www.gurdjiefffourthway. org/pdf/THE%20RAY%20OF%20CREATION.pdf> (Accessed 11/11/2020)

Stang, Charles M. *Our Divine Double.* Cambridge, Massachusetts: Harvard University Press, 2016.

Steindl-Rast, Brother David OSB. "The Body, Sensuousness and Spirituality," lecture at Esalen, 1991. Recording on-line at: <https://gratefulness.org/resource/sensuousness-and-spirituality/> (Accessed 1/10/2021)

Stăniloae, Dumitru. *Orthodox Dogmatic Theology: The Experience of God.* Brookline, Massachusetts: Holy Cross Orthodox Press, 2005.

Strand, Clark, and Perdita Finn. *The Way of the Rose: The Radical Path of the Divine Feminine Hidden in the Rosary.* New York: Spiegel & Grau, 2019.

Strieber, Whitley. *Communion: A True Story.* New York: HarperCollins / William Morrow Paperbacks, reprint edition, 2008.

Swami Chidbrahmananda ("Swami C"). "Vedic Christianity," undated essay at *Vedic Muse* blog. On-line at: <http://vedicmuse.org/wp-content/uploads/2019/09/new-vedic-christianity.pdf> (Accessed 10/5/2020)

Swimme, Brian, and Thomas Berry. *The Universe Story: From the Primordial Flaring Forth to the Ecozoic Era—A Celebration of the Unfolding of the Cosmos.* New York: HarperCollins, 1992, 1994.

Tănase, Nichifor. "Becoming '*all light, all face, all eye*': Central Aspects of Macarius' Theology," *International Journal of Orthodox Theology,* 2018, Volume 9, Issue 4, pp. 32-116. On-line at: <https://www.orthodox-theology.com/media/PDF/4.2018/NichiforTanase.pdf> (Accessed 10/28/2020)

Teasdale, Wayne. *Bede Griffiths: An Introduction to His Interspiritual Thought.* Woodstock, Vermont: SkyLight Paths Publishing, 2003.

Thomas, R. S. *Collected Later Poems 1988-2000.* Tarset, U.K.: Bloodaxe Books, 2013.

Thompson, Robert F. *The Anthropocosmic Vision: For a New Dialogic Civilization.* A Perennials Study Group publication, Memphis, Tennessee (CreateSpace, 2017).

Thompson, Robert F. *From Glory to Glory: The Sophianic Vision of Fr. Sergius Bulgakov.* A Perennials Study Group publication, Memphis, Tennessee. CreateSpace, 2016.

Thompson, Robert F. *Life-Giving Spring: The Eternal Fountain.* A Perennials Study Group publication, Memphis, Tennessee. Kindle Direct Publishing, 2020.

Thompson, Robert F. *Taliesin's Harp: A Poetics of the Divine-Humanity.* A Perennials Study Group publication, Memphis, Tennessee. Kindle Direct Publishing, 2019.

Turner, Philip. *Christian Socialism: The Promise of an Almost Forgotten Tradition.* Eugene, Oregon: Cascade Books / Wipf and Stock Publishers, 2021.

Underhill, Evelyn. *Mysticism: A Study in Nature and Development of Spiritual Consciousness.* Grand Rapids, Michigan: Christian Classics Ethereal Library, first published in 1911. On-line at: <https://ccel.org/ccel/underhill/mysticism/mysticism> (Accessed 1/25/2021)

Unidentified. "On Liminality." A short undated paper in the author's possession from an unknown source.

van Laer, Lee. "Drawn Down Into God." Essay at *Zen, Yoga, Gurdjieff—Perspectives on Inner Work* blog, September 21, 2019. On-line at: <http://zenyogagurdjieff.blogspot.com/2019/09/drawn-down-into-god.html> (Accessed 11/9/2020)

Vaughan-Lee, Llewellyn. *Darkening of the Light: Witnessing the End of an Era.* Point Reyes, California: The Golden Sufi Center, 2013.

Vaziri, Mostafa. *Rumi and Shams' Silent Rebellion: Parallels with Vedanta, Buddhism, and Shaivism.* New York: Palgrave Macmillan, 2015.

Vervaeke, John; Leo Ferraro; and Arianne Herrera-Bennett. "Flow as Spontaneous Thought: Insight and Implicit Learning," in Kalina Christoff and Kieran C.R. Fox, editors, *The Oxford Handbook of Spontaneous Thought: Mind-Wandering, Creativity, and Dreaming*, May 2018. Abstract on-line at: <https://www.oxfordhandbooks.com/view/10.1093/oxfordhb/9780190464745.001.0001/oxfordhb-9780190464745-e-8> (Accessed 9/12/2020)

Vest, Norvene. "Is Reverie to be Trusted? The Imaginal and the Work of Marija Gimbutas," *Feminist Theology*, 2005, Volume 13, Issue 2, pp. 239-248. Preview on-line at: <https://journals.sagepub.com/doi/abs/10.1177/0966735005051950#articleCitationDownloadContainer> (Accessed 10/27/2020)

Vest, Norvene. *Re-visioning Theology: A Mythic Approach to Religion.* Mahwah, New Jersey: Paulist Press, 2011.

Voss, Angela. "Scrying," Chapter 58 in Christopher Partridge, editor, *The Occult World.* New York: Routledge, 2015, 2016. On-line at: <https://mythcosmologysacred.com/wp-content/uploads/2020/08/Scrying.pdf> (Accessed 8/27/2020)

Weil, Simone. Arthur Wills, translator. *The Need for Roots: Prelude to a Declaration of Duties towards Mankind.* London: Routledge, 2002. On-line at: <https://antilogicalism.com/wp-content/uploads/2019/04/need-roots.pdf> (Accessed 9/13/2020)

Welwood, John. "Double Vision: Duality and Nonduality in Human Experience." Essay on-line at: <http://www.johnwelwood.com/articles/DoubleVision.pdf> (Accessed 9/22/2020

Whiting, Marlena. "The Monastic Paradox: negotiating monastic seclusion and pilgrim hospitality in the Late Antique Near East," in *Hypotheses*, an academic blog, October 12, 2016. On-line at: <https://hospitam.hypotheses.org/510> (Accessed 9/12/2020)

Williams, Brendan Ellis. *Seeds from the Wild Verge: Myth, Nature, and Theology in the Border Stream of Celtic Wisdom.* Colorado Springs, Colorado: Ancient Oak Ritual Arts in collaboration with Wandering Words Media, 2020.

Williams, Rowan. *The Way of St. Benedict.* New York: Bloomsbury Continuum, 2020.

Wirtz, Ursula. *Trauma and Beyond: The Mystery of Transformation.* London: Routledge, 2020.

Wisdom, Victoria. "Reverie: A Portal to the Numinous—An Exploration into Early Childhood Psychospiritual Awareness," Ph.D. dissertation, 2014, Pacifica Graduate Institute. On-line at: <https://search.proquest.com/openview/c681be30db0a8f583fac2685cd354796/> (Accessed 10/28/2020)

Yale Forum on Religion and Ecology. On-line at: <https://fore.yale.edu/> (Accessed 1/24/2021)

Zinner, Samuel. *Christianity and Islam: Essays on Ontology and Archetype.* London, U.K.: The Matheson Trust for the Study of Comparative Religion, 2010.

Zwick, Mark and Louise. "Virgil Michel, Benedictine Co-Worker of Dorothy Day and Peter Maurin: Justice embodied in Christ-life and Liturgy," *Houston Catholic Worker*, February 1, 2000. On-line at: <https://cjd.org/2000/02/01/virgil-michel-benedictine-co-worker-of-dorothy-day-and-peter-maurin-justice-embodied-in-christ-life-and-liturgy/> (Accessed 1/9/2021)

About the Author

Robert F. Thompson O.S.B. has wide-ranging and long-standing interest in comparative spirituality, especially transformational teachings from Eastern Christian tradition, Sufism, and other spiritual cultures of both East and West, as well as in Anglican poetic tradition, modern Russian religious thought, spiritual cultures of Central Asia and India, and literature of hesychast experience and tradition. Robert is a member of the Caribbean Philosophical Association.

Blog: http://brightmetaphor.wordpress.com/
Books: https://perennialsstudygroup.wordpress.com/

At Amazon:
https://www.amazon.com/Robert-F.-Thompson/e/B01B50WU74
https://www.amazon.com/dp/1072798573
https://www.amazon.com/dp/1981700978
https://www.amazon.com/dp/1548897965
https://www.amazon.com/dp/1519310722

E-Mail: RThomp2272@yahoo.com